JOSEPH STALIN'S

WINNING MANAGEMENT STRATEGIES FOR THE TWENTY-FIRST CENTURY

Patrick G. Finegan, Jr., Esq.

The Palindrome Press
Washington, DC

This is a work of high fiction. The historical references to the Soviet Union and the factual events surrounding the ascendence to power, life and death of Joseph Stalin have been blended with fiction to produce parody. No reference to living persons has been made or intended, except for communist swine in the Politburo, such as Mikhail Gorbachev and occasinal innocent bystanders in the path of history, such as Stalin's daughter, Svetlana. The Jesuit Order does exist, but no reference is made to any real, living member. It's all fiction. But the point is taken - it could happen again under a different banner.

First Printing

Proudly Printed and Bound in the United States of America.
10 9 8 7 6 5 4 3 2

Finegan, Patrick. G., Jr.

Joseph Stalin's Winning Management Strategies For The Twenty-First Century

ISBN: 1-878905-02-3 HARDCOVER
1-878905-03-1 SOFTCOVER

Library of Congress Catalog Card Number: 90-61774
Fiction.

Dedication

For every good and gentle heart, broken beneath the
onslaught of Scientific Socialism.
There were over 100 million victims in our century.
May God bestow the peace our world cannot.

J.V. Stalin, Official Portrait, 1943, Office of War Information
source: US Library of Congress.

Table of Contents

Deep Background

Stalin's Notes

About the Author
***

Patrick G. Finegan, Jr., Esq.

Attorney Finegan graduated from Fordham College in New York City, then took his JD Law Degree from New York Law School. He next went on to earn a Master of Laws Degree in Corporations from the New York University School of Law, whereupon he served four years as a Captain in the Judge Advocate General Department, United States Air Force, prosecuting and defending Courts Martial and other matters around the world, which he summarizes as a "great four years!"

Next: "Wall Street." He was the Assistant General Counsel for a Member Firm of the New York Stock Exchange for 8 years.

He handled well over 100 securities arbitrations, numerous regulatory investigations and dealt with professionals throughout the financial community on intricate problems. He held numerous securities licenses by the time he left the financial world for private practice:

Registered Representative (Stockbroker)
Associated Person (Commodity Broker)
Registered Options Principal
Branch Manager
Compliance Officer
Supervisory Analyst
General Principal
Financial and Operations Principal
Municipal Securities Principal.

He practices law, writes and lectures in Washington, D.C.

Other Palindrome Books by this author:

MASTER YOUR STOCKBROKER
MASTER FINANCIAL STATEMENTS

PREFACE

In 1848, a wave of change toppled governments throughout Europe and changed the political order of the world. Oddly, the rumblings began in Switzerland. Austria, the political policeman of the area, did not intervene. Within a short time, just to the south, King Ferdinand of Naples was toppled. Monarchy fell to republicanism in northern Italy for the first time, ever.

Next, in France, Emperor Louis Phillipe was torn from his throne by common rabble who fought the Army over barricades in Parisian streets. The fire of the French Revolution was re-ignited.

Modern republics were being born from the corruption of traditional thrones. 1848 has been compared to present events as republicanism is emerging in Eastern Europe, despite years of totalitarian oppression.

In 1847, a young German was living in Brussels, searching for the meaning of life and the goal of political progress. He lived a hard existence of poverty and ostracism because of his radical views. He would soon be ordered out of Belgium, embarking on an odyssey that would take him to Paris, Cologne and London, where he died in March of 1883. In February 1848, he published a small pamphlet, smaller than this book, with a co-author. It was in German, first published in London following a confused convention of political adherents.

An extract from the 1848 pamphlet:

When, in the course of development, class distinctions have disappeared, and all production has been concentrated in the hands of a vast association of the whole nation, the public power will lose its political character. Political power, properly so called, is merely the organized power of one class for oppressing another. If the proletariat during its contest with the bourgeoisie is compelled, by the force of circumstances, to organize itself as a class, if, by means of a revolution, it makes itself the ruling class, and, as such, sweeps away by force the old conditions of production, then it will, along with these conditions, have swept away the conditions for the existence of class antagonisms and of classes generally, and will thereby have abolished its own supremacy as a class.

In place of the old bourgeois society, with its classes and class antagonisms, we shall have an association, in which the free development of each is the condition for the free development of all.

Karl Marx, co-author of the Communist Manifesto along with Frederick Engels, wrote the above extract while steeped in the isolated intensity of ideas that can have a verbal expression but impossible execution. Such rhetorical puzzles are not uncommon. "Can GOD, who is all powerful, make a stone so large that HE cannot move it?" There are many examples of intellectual theories that defy real-world execution. The word "infinity" is an expression. Can we create a physical model of "infinity?"

Marx could not have dreamed up Ulianov (Lenin). In his wildest, darkest nightmares, he could not have dreamed up Djugashvili (Stalin). The Manifesto called for changes in present society that would have built Socialism. The changes that came built nothing but tragedy, consuming lives as the energy of a perverted system.

Ideas are distilled power. They can be deadly in the wrong hands. Perhaps even as you read this, a meek soul is writing a manifesto of political import somewhere in the upheaval of Eastern Europe. He might be writing in Calcutta, Sofia or Vancouver.

Perhaps he is right here in the United States. Take a hard look. Listen. Be prepared. University zealots will claim Marxism was never tested in the Soviet Union, China or anywhere else. They will say 20th century Communism was a "misinterpretation" of Marx. No! Don't accept it. When a snake hisses, preparing to attack you, strike first!

History does not stop. What awaits? Who will be the nightmare of the next century? Under what banner?

PGF, Jr. 12/90.

Official Portrait of V.I. Lenin (Ulianov) used
on a postcard at the Soviet Pavillion, NY World's Fair, 1939.
source: US Library of Congress

FORWARD!

note: Forward - the direction of human endeavor.
Foreword - introductory material for a book.

Palindrome books are usually marked by a distinctive "Forward!" Typically, this is presented as an extract from the writings of a tested philosopher or significant historical figure.

Our author remains absent, absorbed in action elsewhere, as you will soon note. I have no liberty to assume his selection for this work, yet I have an obligation to explain the circumstances. I have finished the manuscript, prepared it for publication and made it available.

Among his notes were several possibilities for this book's "Forward!" One was from the works of Plato, another from Washington's farewell address, still another from the 1803 scaffold speech of Robert Emmet, a famous figure in the Irish struggle for liberty.

At the bottom of the stack of papers, sealed in the metal ammunition box Finegan favors for manuscript delivery, was a well-marked copy of a familiar document. It has hand written parentheses, underlinings and two arrows, in red, highlighting distinct passages. I believe it would be his present selection. He has never done better. It follows:

****

"We hold these truths to be self evident, that all men are created equal, that they are endowed by their Creator with certain unalienable Rights, that among these are Life, Liberty and the pursuit of Happiness. - That to secure these rights, Governments are instituted among Men, deriving their just powers from the consent of the governed,- That whenever any Form of Government becomes destructive of these ends, it is the Right of the People to alter or abolish it, and to institute new Government, laying its foundation on such principles and organizing its powers in such form, as to them shall seem most likely to effect their Safety and Happiness...

...And for the support of this Declaration, with a firm reliance on the protection of Divine Providence, we mutually pledge to each other our Lives, our Fortunes and our Sacred Honor."

****

On a page attached to this text, Finegan had made pencil notes several paragraphs long, then boldly scratched them out with yet another pencil that had a wider, darker lead.

The surviving notes follow in his exact spelling:

"God bless you, Th. Jefferson;

In Congress, July 4, 1776

The Unanimous Declaration of the thirteen united
States of America"

- S. Kopf, A.F.S., Editor.

PART ONE

***

DEEP BACKGROUND

Scott Circle, Massachusetts Ave & 16th St NW,
Washington, DC

Haneman Memorial at Scott Circle, Washington, DC

The Soviet Embassy in Washington, DC, midway between Scott Circle and the White House on 16th St. The Soviets maintain another embassy in New York City for the United Nations.

CHAPTER ONE

THE TEXT
DISCOVERED

As an adolescent, and then a young man, I was educated by the Compania de Jesus, the original title of the Jesuits, at Fordham Preparatory and then Fordham University in New York City.

Over the years, as my life progressed, I lost touch with many of the faculty who had labored far harder than I to change me from a child to a rational man. Some passed to their eternal reward. The Jesuits changed, becoming quite different from the tightly controlled intellectual shock troops of the traditional Roman Catholic Church, which had been their founding standard.

Many Jesuits became caught up in liberation theology in Latin America. Theological and political critics accused them of mixing Marxism with Canon Law, creating a heady mix of bankrupt enthusiasm and detached narcissism.

If I had lost touch with my old teachers, and if, I admit, I reacted to the new, political tilt of the Order with disapproval, I nonetheless remained in contact with a Prep classmate of mine who had joined the

Order years before.

Francis Xavier Bellarmine. I called him Francis or "FX" as his old, school nickname.

My memories of my old friend were delightful. Once, in school, he ate a light bulb upon a dare. Many years ago when gangsters and bootleggers made headlines during the prohibition era (1920's), young braggarts ate goldfish, alive, swallowing them whole, at a gulp. As times change, other variations of daring fads occur. When I was 16, the rage was light bulbs. FX cracked the delicate glass on a cafeteria tabletop, picked up the sharp glass pieces, and, staring all the while with bright, blue eyes at his taunting adversary, ground the shards to sand with his powerful bite and perfect teeth. He refrained from consuming the metal base and the internal filament with the theatrical disdain of an immortal.

We thought he would die. I wondered, even as FX was grinding away, how we would deliver his agonized body to his mother, how we would describe the situation that had taken on the proportion of myth and led to teenage death at the hands of adolescent ignorance - but he lived!

He flourished!

He was one of the strongest, craziest boys I knew. Excellent in Latin, fluent in Greek, it was Russian that brought his eventual downfall. But, let me not race ahead.

I remember him lifting weights to further develop his steeled biceps. He would stand and gently lift 20 pounds, an arm at a time, 10 repetitions to a set, with a short rest between sets. After 4 sets, his muscles would complain, the arm would become tired. But, he would press on to the point of pain. When pain began, he would recite Russian poetry, maintaining the repetitions until he finished one complete set in physical agony, grunting unrecognizable verse until he dropped the weight to its rest and howled with athletic intensity, cursing away in literate Bronx hyperbole. The teenage years are made of magic, inspiring us throughout our lives.

By all standards, he was a regular fellow, a good friend, a kid who could be trusted with the greatest confidences. In college, about the second year, the time when unwelcome responsibility seeps into a student's life as one decides a major course of study, he felt God's calling. He "enlisted" in the "Societas Jesu." We stayed in touch for the next decade, talking and writing to each other. His commitment was genuine, growing each year.

The Jesuits require a long course of preparation as a prelude to ordination. As much as fifteen years can be spent in arduous study and self examination in the pursuit of sufficient merit to be ordained.

The typical preparation first involves a few years as a novice, usually two, concentrating on academics. Then three vows are taken: chastity, poverty and obedience.

The next decade is spent as a "Scholastic." Many Scholastics teach in Jesuit schools around the world. They are addressed as "Mister," not "Father." In the Roman Catholic Church, ordination is the final step. It is the moment where a man becomes a priest, dedicating his life to the service of God. A priest's life is not his own. It belongs, in faith and devotion, to the Lord, pledged to God's service without reserve, condition, or end.

FX took a special fourth vow of devoted, personal

obedience to the Pope upon ordination. While this is outwardly symbolic, it can be fundamentally and personally powerful. It is what the Jesuit Order is all about.

The Jesuits had been started as an almost military group. They began in Paris as an association of six university students. The Spanish word "Compania" denotes a traditional infantry unit. They received their Charter from Pope Paul the Third in 1540. Ignatius Loyola, the Jesuit founder, was named the "General" of the then-small order in 1541.

Jesuit history has been intertwined with Europe's political machinations from the outset. The Jesuits opposed the extreme financial and physical oppression of the colonies by the crowned capitalists of France and Spain. New World gold from Central and South America was secured at a horriffic price in human life. The Jesuits would not back down in their defense of the native population. But, they could not stop a bureaucratic ambush from behind, in Rome. France, Spain and Portugal were ultimately successful in persuading Pope Clement the Fourteenth to disband the order in 1773.

Fractured Europe brought Jesuit salvation. While they were driven from their birthplace in Paris, Pope Clement's edict was not accepted in Eastern Germany by Frederick the Great or in Russia by Catherine the Great, daughter and successor of Tsar Peter the Great. These two, political giants knew what the Pope had ordered, but they would not allow publication of the dissolution edict in their respective kingdoms, thus creating territorial loopholes preventing Jesuit extinction.

Ultimately, in 1814, Pope Pius the Seventh restored the Jesuits, revoking Pope Clement's futile effort. Thereafter, the Jesuits became Europe's great educators.

Catherine and Frederick had saved them.

While Frederick had arguable political motives because of his extreme dislike for the French, Catherine's was an act of magnanimous grace because Russia's State Religion was not Roman Catholicism, but that 800 year old miracle, the Russian Orthodox Church. She had no personal or political debt to the Jesuits and could have ignored them.

Perhaps she acted under the influence of her father, the great Tsar Peter. His thirst for knowledge and affection for progressive Western ideas led to the creation of the great city of Petrograd or, as we call it today, Leningrad. Catherine stood behind a theological underdog.

The Jesuits, therefore, have always had a special attachment to Mother Russia. Despite their outward profession of obedience, they maintain a strange, political relationship with the Vatican. The past is not forgotten. Although "it" happened over two hundred years ago, Jesuits know they once were at the edge of a vast theological abyss.

FX, as I knew him, was not politically inclined until shortly before we lost contact. He did not support specific political candidates during his Scholastic years. He was a moderate Democrat. We differed, poles apart, on Vietnam. When I went to law school, he was ministering to the poor in southern Mexico. When I was in the US Air Force, he was teaching in a small village in Nicaragua. I was in South Korea when he was ordained in the New York Province, after which he returned to Nicaragua.

While I could not be there to witness his vows, I
sent him an original Meerlug pocket bible, first edition,
Munich, 1735. I had gotten it as a gift from my Grand
Aunt who had been a member of the corps de ballet,
then a prima donna of the Danse de Monaco in the
1920's. She had developed a scandalous celebrity for
her collections of husbands and jewels. Toward the end
of her life, she settled down. Eventually, upon her
death, she left the husbands to history, the jewels to
the Church and the bible to me because I was the only
one who admired her art and company with equal
fascination, even when she had become old.

I respected FX for the serious mission he had
pledged. Theological adventure requires a full life of
service to distill the intensity of conviction required to
meet great challenge.

He was deeply affected by the relentless poverty in
the Latino third world and by the Anglo ignorance of
where this misery would inevitably lead.

He began to quote Karl Marx in his letters to me
as frequently as Thomas Aquinas or Francis Borgia. He
suffered the anguish of frustration that tortures passionate minds when positive action is politically
forbidden. He was like an athlete bound with restrain-
ts, struggling to break free.

And then he disappeared.

In August, 1980, his letters stopped. I made casual,
then more urgent inquiry. Finally, I heard from contacts in the New York Province that FX had departed
his Nicaraguan village on pastoral rounds and had not
come back. No one knew where he had gone.

No one suggested he might have voluntarily
deserted his post. Rather, the suspicion was that he
had been assassinated by one political group or anoth-

er during the Sandinista turmoil, then left in the bush, dead. Disappearances were commonplace in that area. People vanished, traces unknown, embraced by the earth in shallow, jungle graves.

He was gone.

I felt the sorrow associated with mourning a friend's death, but without the consolation of seeing him receive Catholic burial. As I look back, I felt cheated. I missed him. It cuts close when a childhood friend dies. Anger and frustration mix with sorrow in tides of emotion. It would wash over me at the strangest times. Such a noble man. Such a sudden disappearance.

Years passed.

It's true - time does heal wounds.

As I moved in my career and life, the pain faded and my adolescent memories matured. I thought of FX as I had last seen him, years before he disappeared: exuberant, motivated, strong as a bull, full of promise. It was a marvelous enrichment of my life. Perhaps that had been God's purpose. Perhaps FX was destined to live, inspire, and leave his subtle mark in the most powerful way, in the hearts of his friends and family.

Our lives grasp a moment of fleeting, direct impact, but the resonance of our actions lingers, spreading like waves upon the sea of life, until all is merged, anonymous, into the great reality.

I had no demonstrable, real evidence to prove him dead, but I believed he had died. The Jesuits told me they thought so, too. I knew shadow people in the area - my sources reported they found nothing, heard nothing. My inquiries had been casual, but continuous, made with old friends who owed favors.

One night, three months ago, I received a telephone call at my office in Washington, DC. As the hour was late, I was alone, working. The telephone buzzed it's electronic signal ten times before I decided a crank was relentlessly demanding an answer. I let it go on, wishing I had remembered to engage the answering machine. The caller was not going to hang up.

I could ignore it no longer, so I picked up the receiver, managing an attempt at mild disapproval in my cold "hello."

A cough. A second, lighter cough. Then he said, "Padraig, d'you think we might (cough) talk." I didn't move, but my mind fell back as though I was stumbling. I knew the voice! Years passed instantly. Distance dissolved as I felt a lightness in my upper chest.

I knew it! I knew the feeble attempts at a rich Irish brogue, imitating a Jesuit, now many years dead, who had taught a class of young boys the way Latin was REALLY pronounced.

I had been in that class. So had FX. Freshman year in our ancient building. My desk was as old as the Ark. It had "Mick class of '10" carved inside under the top wooden lid. Oh yes, an old school with old desks that tied students to a century's traditions in a building covered with ivy and boyhood dreams. He sat, captive at the next desk, beside me. He thought the Irish Father McGuinn a linguistic challenge while the rest of us thought him a classical bore.

I recovered quickly and spoke softly into the receiver, as though whispering a secret to a close confidant. "Francis, where are you? Where can I meet you?"

He quietly answered, "look out your window, across and down Sixteenth Street, toward the White House. It's I."

Grammatically correct, as ever. I peered between slats of the venetian blind, through windows covered with sheets of rain and city soot.

I saw him, a silhouette a block away at an outdoor telephone short of Scott Circle in front of a small inn. He waved. I knew he couldn't see me as clearly as I could see him, because of the wind and rain. I felt his wave was an act of faith. He knew I would look. He trusted me to look.

I felt an odd premonition. I didn't recognize it then, but I do now, with the luxury of hindsight and time to think. He waved without being able to see me, because he knew I would look.

Still holding the telephone, I told him to come up and get out of the rain. He cut me off and said, "No, can't. Come downstairs and meet me over on Seventeenth in the Chinese joint off Mass Ave," speaking like a Republican Washingtonian who flinches at the full sound of "Massachusetts."

"Francis," I began to object,"it's raining too hard. Come over. I'll grab my coat. We'll get a cab and go over to Georgetown - "

He cut me off. "Oh, Padraig," he said quietly and seriously, continuing to use the Gaelic pronunciation for Patrick, "If you have one handy, you might want to bring rough company." An old New York expression.

I was silent. He wasn't joking. While not melodramatic, he was making a point to scatter my objections and grab my attention.

It worked.

I knew he was serious. He hung up as I stared ahead, seeing myself reflected in the wet office window. The click of his disconnect was an affirmation, a brief declaration of trust that I would meet him.

I put my telephone down. Briefs, books and stacks of loose references were everywhere in my office, all over the desk, the floor and a few tables. I was working on a complex securities case involving phoney balance sheets, "cooked books," and a crooked brokerage house. I sat in my chair, took off my bifocals and rubbed my eyes.

One hand's fingertips lightly drummed the worn mahogany desk top, the other massaged my late-day, stubble chin.

It was Francis. He was back! But, from where?

I wondered what I should do. I had a choice: I could sit in the dry comfort of my office or I could dash out in the rain, into the unknown. I had no time to debate the matter. He was waiting. Time confuses decisions that a true heart would command. I knew what to do.

My "dead" Jesuit friend wanted me to meet him, armed, for a purpose that had to be worthy. Had he really called? Was I working too hard? One long breath; another. I thought about another school, not at all like the comfortable womb of adolescence.

I shifted in the chair, reaching to the lower right hand desk drawer, pulling it open in a slow movement, trying to avoid any sound. Metal lined wood glided on stainless steel ball bearings, stopping when the reinforced drawer was fully extended. At the back, under a mixture of papers, plastic spoons, needles and thread, ancient pencils and stale candy, I felt the strongbox welded to the metal drawer liner.

I worked the combination lock and removed the padded, plastic case. I opened the black velcro fastener with a stark tearing sound and reached inside.

Years ago, far away, I learned that walking into a

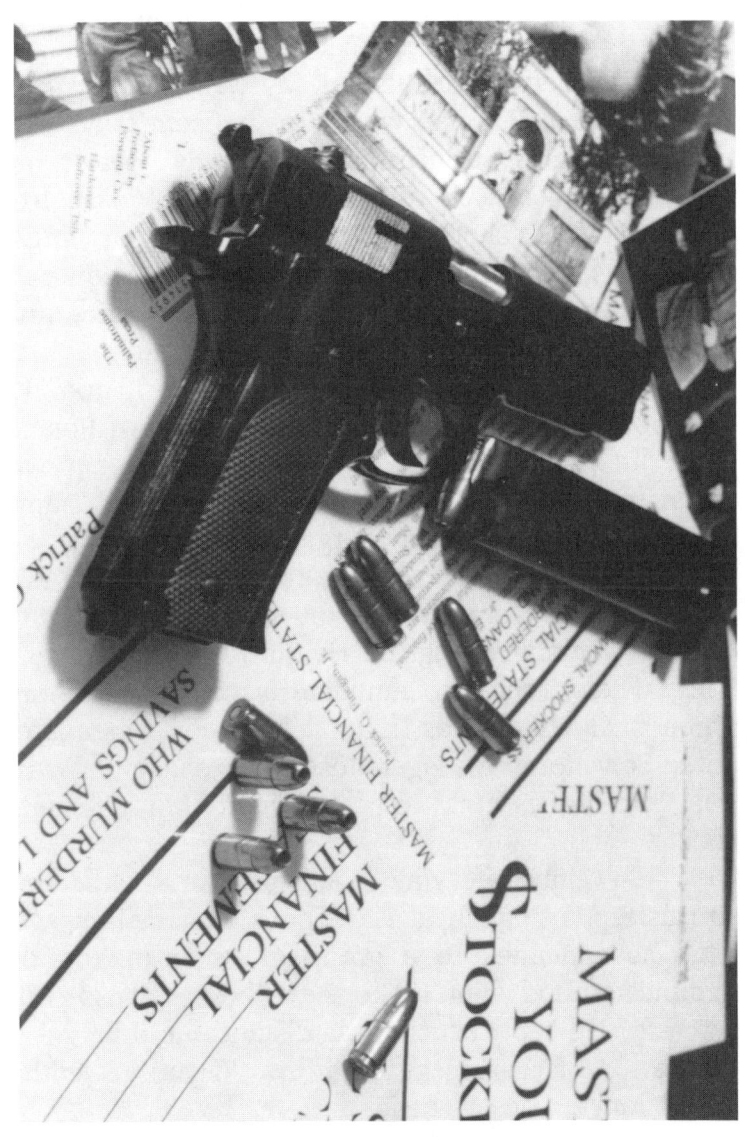

Rough Company

gun fight was stupid. It was jungle Panama, in a special school where the students and faculty used an assigned first name, carried no identification, and spoke only German or Russian. My weapons instructor was a quiet, small man with a magnificent moustache that hid a large surgical scar. US Army doctors had sewn his lip back on after East German Volkspolizei had just about shot it off while he was climbing a fence at Marienborn. His false teeth were too white for his mottled complexion. I learned his real name only years later, after he was killed in El Salvador.

Many of his students owed much to "Turk." He was born a German in what is now western Poland. Prior to 1945 it was part of East Prussia, but was given to Poland as part of World War Two's "adjustments." He was Helmut Morgen.

Before defecting, he was a top trainer for the East German Stasi Organization, the muscle of that now-defunct Communist regime. He quit, turned, and came West when ordered to liquidate a man, his wife and three small children as traitors. Ironically, years later, three Salvadoran teenagers tossed a grenade under his cab, turning a vital, respected man into butchered meat.

"The only safe way to kill people is while they are asleep, using nuclear weapons from a long way off," he explained to a group of us sitting on the ground around him. "The next best way is with aircraft." He kept reducing the distance until he got to the lesson of close-in gun fighting. "If you get within pistol range, you are dead."

"Convince yourself that you are already dead, a victim of your own stupidity for getting that close with only a handgun." It was an interesting perspective. He continued, "the best weapon close in is a pump shotgun. Close fast, fire twice, finish with a coup de grace to the head. Small machine pistols will scatter rounds, and you will probably run out of ammunition just at the point you have been hit by your own ricochet or killed your comrades with wild shooting."

His instruction had the abrupt precision of experience. If you had to walk into a gun fight, then start by accepting your own death. If you were dead, what else could happen?

If you were hit by a round, get up. Dead men cannot be dropped. If you are bleeding, don't worry. You are already dead. If you are hurt, keep going. Dead men can't be hurt.

Stay away from gun fights. Get someone else to do it. Run from it. Think around it. Bribe your way out, claw your way out, hide, then escape.

If there was no other way, then start by being dead. When you could plan, Turk advised using two semi-automatic 9mm pistols with extended magazines, provided you have large enough hands to carry the grip a little further down. Shotguns are just too bulky for concealment.

Gun fights could only take place on a city street, inside an aircraft, a building, a train or other confined space. In an open field, never. Run away, use a rifle, use explosives - don't use a pistol in an open field. You will be embarrassed, as you are cut down by trained professionals.

On the street, the plan was simple. First, be dead. Then decide the time of your advantage. Have one magazine in your left pocket, if right handed. Draw weapons. Dump the first round from each, no matter if using double action or cocking pistols. This meant the first rounds were used to get ready for serious shooting. The first rounds cause most people to turn toward you with noise reflexes, giving clear, recognizable targets, frozen in place by fear.

Once fired, the semi-automatic pistol chambers a new round and cocks itself. The second shot requires a much lighter trigger pull. If you were using twenty round magazines, 38 shots were left. With everyone's attention focused on the pistols, you are in control - but only as long as you mean business. They will see the weapons, not your face. Their neck muscles will tighten, fixing their attention on you. Adrenalin will pump, telling them to run away, if they can move at all - except professionals; they will stand and fight.

Isolate your target. Even if you have more than one, go after one at a time. Believe you can't be hurt. Walk right up to the target. Keep firing. Don't stop.

As soon as you stop, you lose momentum. Your muzzle blast and flash will leave you temporarily deaf, but it will stop your opponent from being able to concentrate to fire on you. Fill his sight with your fire, closing in. Don't just look at him - aim at him. Kill him.

Close and kill.

Practice your pace. Think of music, not your firing. Fire three rounds with your left hand for noise and blast. Then fire seriously with your right. 3,1; 3;1, keep walking.

If your left hand shots are successful, you are lucky. Aim the left low. It will rise naturally as you fire. Shoot the knees with the left. The knees have no armor and as your fire rises you may hit the chest or head. If you miss with the right, you are a fool. Snap the left. Aim the right. Don't stop walking forward, don't stop firing. 3,1; 3,1; walk, walk, walk. You are already dead.

Now cut the target down. Close and kill. Don't stop.

Turn to the next target. Walk, 3;1; 3,1. When the left hand pistol goes empty, drop it, fire with the right. Get the extra magazine ready. Keep walking. Fire with each step. Don't run.

When the right hand goes dry, the slide will stop "back," waiting for you to eject the spent magazine, insert the new one, thumb the slide free, and continue walking and firing. It takes one step.

If you get to your opponent but have not cut him down, do whatever it takes. If you can't cut down two men with 60 deliberate rounds, you deserve to die. You WILL be dead.

Practice, practice and practice. Day, night, twilight. Walk. Don't run. Think of music. You are dead. Dump rounds. 3,1; 3,1. Walk. Left hand dry. Walk, walk.

The whole drill takes about 25 seconds for the full sixty rounds. You can cover thirty paces, about the length of three cars. Thirty rounds should be within small target circles on the opponent. Center chest and always, always the forehead to make sure about body armor.

Practice, practice and practice.

It never goes completely away. Practice until it is reflex. No thought - reflex. No fear - reflex. Jumping a horse, skiing on ice, catching second wind while running a fast mile - training and reflex. Once learned, it remains, forever.

I pulled two Smith and Wesson 59's from the case, each in a separate, oil-hazed freezer bag. From the old days.

I gently removed them from their bags and removed the excess oil with my handkerchief, depositing the handkerchief back in one bag. The machine oil smell was distant and familiar. Panama. Twilight. I passed the 64th test in 20 seconds. I was the only one who could shoot the left and right for accuracy. I throw with the right hand but kick with the left foot. I fire with both hands, snap or aim.

I put the plastic bags back in the case, dropping the black shape back into the desk drawer. One minute had passed.

I reached down into the drawer and got the three magazines, as fat, but slightly longer than the normal ones. 20 rounds each, with specially tempered, constant pressure, stainless steel springs. Jacketed hollow point, 115 gr., P+ rounds.

The Smith is a double action pistol. No cocking like a Browning Hi-Power or Government Colt. It's a reliable combat side arm. A stiff pull on the first, dumped round gives a ready, velvet touch of accurized firepower for each round that follows.

Never slam a magazine into a pistol. Push it in gently. Press until it clicks. As I loaded, I thought about FX and wondered what might happen in the next hour. I had plenty of questions, but he was my friend and a priest.

"Why me?" No, it was more a question of why me and a weapon - why not the police? DC overflows with police of all kinds. Why me? I had no answer. But, I didn't need an answer. He was my friend.

Professionals routinely carry the Smith with a full magazine, but no round in the chamber, until ready for action. It's a belt and suspenders approach to safety. If there is no round in front of the firing pin, you can drop it, abuse it, pull the trigger - "it won't go off accidentally in your pants, punching a hole right through your prize anatomy," Turk said.

I didn't know what was going to happen. I pulled back the slide, felt the spring resist, then slowly let the slide come forward, pushing a bullet from the magazine into the breech of the 4-inch barrel. The hammer was down. Loaded. Safety, "off."

I got ready to go.

I carried a Smith in each outside pocket of my trenchcoat. I didn't turn the lights out. I didn't turn the computers off. It didn't matter.

Hand guns are illegal in Washington, DC, but not for everyone. You never really retire from my former outfit, remaining in a very unheralded reserve for life.

As I stepped out onto Sixteenth, the rain slowed. I wanted to rush over to Seventeenth, but you can't run with pistols in a raincoat, so I walked quickly along "P" Street, hands inside.

Water flew from puddles as cabs ripped past, cruising for late fares, racing around a slow, loud Metrobus. I calmed myself on the noisy street. I was getting dead, reaching for that old skill. Nothing bad can happen. It has already happened. You are unstoppable. You don't have to be brave; nothing can happen. It returned.

I travelled across "P" Street, then down on Seventeenth. As I was about to enter Fong's, I felt a presence come up behind me. Old instincts. Did I hear anything? Instinct let's you "feel" beyond the range of deliberate senses. I turned. A tired, soft voice met me half-way, "let's walk."

He coughed a few times, not loudly, but deeply, trying to hold lung pressure down by light, rapid breathing as though a regular breath would bring more coughing. We walked a hundred feet. His breathing cleared. He spat onto the wet street.

We walked down Seventeenth, then left along Massachusetts, around Scott Circle toward the Statue of Haneman, the founder of Osteopathic Medicine. The rain decreased to a drizzle.

Even though we had not written or spoken to each other for years, and even though he must have known I thought him murdered, we didn't speak for a few minutes as we walked.

I reasoned he would talk when he chose.

He was thinner than I had ever seen him, stooped at the shoulder. His blue eyes, which moved rapidly about, scanning all directions, had large, dark circles around them. Grey replaced his red hair. I was older and far softer; he was older and worn. He was tired. I don't mean physically, the way an athlete refreshes after a burst of exertion, the way a boxer collapses onto his stool, then jumps up to get back in the ring at the sound of the bell. He was wheezing and holding himself with a tension I knew resulted from mental and physical exhaustion. He was beaten. By what? Why?

With his left hand, he carried an expandable, schoolboy briefcase made of old, black leather. Its appearance was reassuringly academic. The leather was napping up with age at the stitched seams on the top and sides. The handle was frayed. There was a red, star-shaped insignia on the single closure strap at the top, center, but it was worn past clarity. It was, in all respects, ordinary. The slow drip of blood gliding over his wet fingers grasping the handle, coming from underneath his black raincoat and mixing with the rain on his knuckles, was extraordinary.

Without staring, I saw no entry wound on his coat, front or back. Whatever its origin, the loss of blood, while noticeable, was slight. He was strong enough to carry the case. He kept the other hand, his right hand, in his filled, right raincoat pocket. Was he armed, too? Why?

We strolled along, two men in the rain at 11 PM on a Wednesday night, he with a briefcase, me with a hat.

The city, at night in winter, was ours. We proceeded on now-empty streets.

"Thank you, my friend," he said quietly, as we walked, finally breaking our silence. "It's been a while." I nodded, knowing he had far more to say.

"You have children, I understand."

"Yes," I replied. It's odd how people can measure the worth of life in a few words. The elegance of expression is often its brevity, life amplifying meaning by experience, not words.

A few moments passed. Then he gave me a brief glimpse of his recent life. "Please, listen," he almost ordered, "there isn't time to chat. I need your help, tonight. I need to talk. I have sinned, I am in trouble, and I need your friendship."

He stopped walking. We looked at each other, old friends. "Then tell me," I said, assuring him by those few words of my commitment.

We walked to the Haneman memorial, which is a small granite structure with a historic mosaic of the great doctor's life and accomplishments. The side facing Scott Circle has a miniature built-in bench and follows the graceful curve of an open ellipse. There are no separate benches in front. "Die Milde Macht ist Gross," says one engraving. So it is. Further down, at the end of Sixteenth, the White House was aglow with halogen security lights.

We sat on the wet granite. The monument wrapped us in it's curve and gave us a cover of thick stone from behind and a 165 degree field of fire to the front over clear lawns. It was a good place for a defensive action, but open to even medium quality parabolic microphone surveillance. All Washington is surveilled by paras.

We sat. He composed himself and told me a brief story.

HIS STORY IN HIS WORDS

"As you know, I speak seven languages well enough that anyone would think me a native. It's a great, but terrible gift.

In the late 1970's, Mexico and Latin America were under financial pressure to pay off unbearable loans to North American and European Banks. The actual loan funds had since been squandered in governmental and business corruption, so the debtors had nothing to pay with. Nothing had been built that was producing revenue from the loan proceeds. Government officials had taken the loans, and then bought expensive homes in London, Paris, Southern California, and Connecticut. Gringo bankers wanted payments. There was no money left.

No businesses had been built.

Latin governments decided to squeeze money out of those who could afford it least, but who could also resist the least: the unorganized peasants.

Soviet-style Communism was blossoming to the

south, once again in contradiction to Marx's model of industrial society as the prime Revolutionary vanguard. The peasants from the countryside were beginning to mass, opposed to central governments linked to the United States.

Peasants don't choose Communism as an ideal. They will, however, accept it as the only alternative to pending, certain starvation. They would accept extraterrestrials on those same terms.

In 1979, I met a special envoy from Rome, who arrived in Managua by way of Helsinki and Portugal, one of those damn Italian Bishops - this one called D'Albret, a French name. He was always travelling.

You may have heard of him. French father, Italian mother from Milano, both dead from the Second World War. He brought introductions from two cardinals I knew in the US. He didn't wear a cassock, favoring a fitted dark suit, a gray shirt and thin blue tie. He had tiny feet and wore patent leather shoes.

Our brief meeting took place at the Mendano Airport, the old one on the western edge of Managua. We sat outdoors at a small cafe drinking strong, local coffee. He smoked several Gaulois.

He indicated he had heard of me because of a translation of Nietzsche I had made from German into Spanish and Russian for a BBC broadcast into Cuba in 1979.

While I was flattered by the notoriety, Nietzsche is not a difficult translation. I knew there had to be more than languages causing the long trip and meeting. The Pope himself spoke four languages. D'Albret and I spoke in French and Italian during our discussion. We rambled back and forth about politics in Central America and life, or what passes for life, in the

Eternal City.

We came to silence, the formalities past.

Then he asked me about my fourth vow. What did I think of it? Was it sincere? Would I undertake a mission from the Vatican in deepest confidence? Did I trust the Vatican?

When I asked if our General was aware of the conversation, he smiled and sat back, looking at me. He waited only a moment, and asked, "does it matter?" Is your fourth vow to your General or your Pope?

I didn't answer, because I haven't much use for Italian Bishops who politic their way around the Vatican like worms spoiling good fruit. They have smooth hands and occasionally wear too much cologne, as if to affect an effeminate air in a male bastion. Our discussion ended with cold respect.

I told him I would not agree to further discussion, much less a decision, without the knowledge of my Order. Inwardly, I wanted more than the word of an Italian bishop.

About a month later, I again met with a visiting dignitary, this time Thomas Dunne Porro, a senior Jesuit from the New York Province. Porro was 78 years old then. I had met him many times at dinner and other social occasions, though I never studied under him. He was nominally retired. Officially, he was in Managua to see his aged cousin Helena and visit surviving friends from his mission days. He had emphysema, but continued to chain smoke. Travel was not easy.

When we met at the Order's house in Managua, he took me aside to a small chapel on the ground floor, behind the large library-reception room. We sat facing each other on worn wooden chairs as the Pascal

Candle flickered in the semi-dark. He wore his collar in the old style, making me feel self-conscious in my open-necked cotton shirt. His large eyes were filled with red capillaries, but they maintained an impish twinkle that I found endearing and inspiring. This was a man who had travelled and touched the world.

"I am passing, Francis," he said. "My life has been blessed in the service of God." He looked deeply into my own eyes.

"There is a man in Rome who needs your service," he told me. "Our General asked me to tell you that you have freedom to agree or not to this man's request. It is a matter of your conscience and heart. Our General and this man agree on this matter."

Porro took my hand in his tough, cool grip and continued, "If I had the strength, I would serve this cause." He was brief, but he made his point.

I thanked him and pledged further thought.

We went to dinner with the others. I understood the urgency without knowing the mission. Porro died shortly after returning to New York, active to the end. His words remained in my daily thoughts.

A month after that, the Italian D'Albret returned and we met at the same house. We sat together, in private, but in the brightly lit treasury office. He swore me to secrecy and asked if I was ready to serve. I agreed because of Porro's assurance. D'Albret still used the distinctive cologne.

He asked if I had extensive knowledge of Karl Marx.

I switched from Italian to German and recited from the Manifesto. My favorite quote from Marx, however, is from the famous eleventh thesis contra Feuerbach, "Die Philosophen haben die Welt nur

verscheiden interpretiert, es kommt darauf an, sie zu
verändern." (The Philosophers have only interpreted
the world. It's up to us to change it.)

"Excellent," D'Albret replied. You already know
more about building Socialism than Castro and these
Sandinista pigs," said D'Albret. When I asked how he
came to that conclusion, he answered sharply that at
least I could read and had studied their intellectual
master, more than most of the Communists in Latin
America or in my own Jesuit Order.

The mission was simple enough: I was to begin
showing signs of discontent with Church Dogma and
North American treatment of the Latin American debt
question. I could do this by speaking, writing - however I chose. It had to start, then build up. Rome expected I would then be recruited.

They weren't sure by whom, Castro, the locals or
the Soviets, but that was the challenge. The Church
did not want to be caught reacting to theological revolution when it had the opportunity to tap into the
Communist thought processes and watch a full recruiting effort.

Because I spoke fluent Spanish and Russian, and
because I was an American, Rome thought I would
prove irresistible, that the Communists would show
every trick they had to get me on their side. I could
then advise the Vatican on ways to counter recruiting,
indoctrination and long term plants in the Church.

It worked.

A few of the letters I sent you were part of that
plan. I knew my mail was being opened. I apologize,
but I knew it wouldn't harm you, because you were
leaving the shadows. I made speeches. I wrote posters
and pamphlets. I even wrote a Maoist revolutionary

opera.

Eventually, I was invited to dinner by the other side. I must hurry.

In August, 1980, I had to leave Nicaragua abruptly, because they wanted me to choose: join or not. The recruiting was not a dance - it was direct.

Following my Papal mission, I agreed to join the Revolution.

Immediately, I was sent to Patrice Lumumba University in Moscow, via Havana where I became a hidden, training resident for several years. I wasn't just recruited. I was supposed to study, train and then coordinate the anti-clergy program on a worldwide basis, attempting to place reliable contacts inside the Church hierarchy who would work for the Revolution now and for the next fifty years.

The Soviets felt the present dissatisfaction with the strict tenets of our faith was an opportunity that was temporary and had to be exploited before it disappeared. If operatives were in place quickly, they could remain effective for a long time.

Late in 1980 they told me to travel around the Soviet Union, to consider it my new home. I spent months with two travelling companions from the KGB's Fourth Directorate. They urged me to get married to a nice Russian girl. I didn't.

I took in the sights, travelling east to visit the boyhood home of V. I. Lenin (Ulianov), west to visit the battlefields of World War Two, south to study the Moslem minority, and southwest, on a special trip to see St. Basil's, outside the small town of Gori. I saw the canals in Leningrad, factories in Kursk and Murmansk, and I went fishing just north of Vladivostok on the Pacific. It was terminally boring because the more you travel in the Soviet Union, the less attractive it is. The geography can be stunning, but the manifestations of man reflect the failure of an artificial system. People sleepwalk through their lives because there is little to stir the intellect.

Thousands of miles and several months passed.

I did pseudonymous broadcasts for Radio Moscow, translations of garbage, stressing midwest "r's" in their North American English Language Service. I believed they were trying to test me by boring me to submission, then snapping a psychological trap. I was almost ready. Then, in May, 1981, they almost killed the Pope, right in St. Peter's Square! My life continued.

Much later, in November, 1983, I got a call from a mid-level apparatchik I knew over at the Kremlin Central Committee Offices. He said that we should meet by the Beklimeshev Tower which is part of the Kremlin Wall, next to the Moscow River.

I walked from my office in the basement of the State Historical Museum, on the other side of the Lenin Mausoleum, along Red Square, past the parked Intouirist busses, to meet Sergei Anatoly Kiralnov. It was cold, but clear.

A pleasant day for a fast walk. It was noon. Crowds were out waiting to view Lenin's remains, strolling, talking in small clusters or organized in large tours. I didn't meet Kiralnov. I waited at the Tower for fifteen minutes, until a man approached me, asking if I had a match.

He didn't have a cigarette.

He chewed a wooden match as though it was a toothpick. The soft pulp was split and wet as it stuck slightly from the side of his mouth. The yellow sulphur tip was dry, indicating a practiced touch, probably of a man trying to quit smoking lung-busting Russian cigarettes which, according to the popular humor, were made from grass clippings now that there was a shortage of fresh horse manure.

I told him no, that I didn't have any matches. He responded by saying it was a nice day and we should talk. His features were southern, broad shouldered, olive skin, thick brown hair and eyebrows. He had a gold-backed front tooth in the Russian style. He scared the daylights out of me by his assured manner.

He spit out the old match, replacing it with another, twirling it from one side of his mouth to the other.

He told me that he was from the KGB's Fifth Directorate and that he knew I was planted in their system through a counter-intelligence plan that originated in the Vatican several years ago.

I expected to die right there or in a short time. I was prepared, almost relieved. They'd grab me, take me off. One shot in the back of the head, in the old style. But it wasn't that easy.

He told me more.

There was disagreement within the government over the shooting of the Pope. Questions of control, power and the future had sprung out of the genie's bottle and could not be put back. Things were going to change. Radical difference was possible as evolving sides were being taken, anticipating the Party Secretary's death and the final grasp of the Old Bolshevik hold on the Central Committee of the Communist Party of the Soviet Union.

I listened. I had no choice, but I was also fascinated. Fifth Directorate did not talk to targets; they used to kill them.

We switched from Russian to English. He had a terrible, heavy accent, but wanted to impress me. "You have several hours to get out of the Soviet Union. We aren't interested in you, but tomorrow, the Fourth Directorate will come, and probably shoot you, unless they interrogate for a few days first."

I was ready to leave right then.

He had more to say, "All you have to do is take this briefcase with you to the West, today. You will go to London. 4 PM flight out. Stay at the DeGaulle Hotel. Don't wander around too much. After three days, a man will come to you. A priest, like you. From the Vatican. Give him the case. Then go and live your life back in America. If you don't follow these instructions, we'll find you and kill you. If we can't find you, we'll kill your mother. If you go back to Nicaragua, we'll find you there, too. All the papers and tickets you need are in this envelope." He reached into his coat and produced a creased, used, yellow envelope, putting it in my left hand.

"Why me," I calmly asked as I looked at the envelope with quiet terror.

"Because you are a priest and the man you will give this to is a priest. We don't have many priests readily available, not ones trusted in Rome. You are known to Rome. My Directorate does not want war with the angels. We did not try to hurt Rome. Deliver this case."

He meant they did not try to shoot the Pope.

"What's in the case," I asked.

"No. That doesn't concern you. It's just paper. Rome wants it. We want them to have it. There is no copy of these papers. They come from the KGB's deep vaults under the Lenin Hills, outside Moscow. Oh yes, if you lose the papers, we'll kill you. Just take them. Give them to the priest who comes for them and no one will bother you."

"Can you guarantee my safety?"

He shrugged. "Life has no guarantees. I will try to help you. I think I can do it. Priest, I could be gone tomorrow. The country is changing. Anyway, does it matter? If you don't do this, you will be dead by tomorrow night. You must go today."

We stopped. He handed me the plain briefcase. "Who will the priest be," I asked.

"I don't know," he shrugged, "that's Rome's authority, not mine." Without shaking hands, without any further words, he turned and walked back toward Red Square, as casual as any tourist, except he wore comfortable western shoes that fit and were polished.

I waited a few moments, more in shock than to allow him to leave alone. I had no idea what was in the bag. What would Rome want? It couldn't be military secrets. It couldn't be scientific or other breakthroughs. What? What would the Vatican want? What would the Soviets give up, with no copy left behind.

In Moscow, back then, everything was seen; everything was heard. I felt a hundred eyes follow me as I walked back into Red Square, returning to my office.

Suddenly, I realized that to get on a four o'clock flight, I had to go direct to the airport, without delay. I hurried. There was nothing to wait for, nothing to miss. They knew about me. How did they know? Three years of effort and nothing. They wasted my time, yet made the Vatican feel my mission had been productive.

Finnair took me on the first leg -I thought- home.

I slept. The briefcase rested under my feet. We stopped in Helsinki, then moved on to Paris. I changed there and flew to London. No one in Customs bothered to even look in my one piece of baggage, the case. Travellers still can't find anything to smuggle out of the Soviet Union. There is little worth buying. Customs officers rush you along to get to more serious business, their break time.

The DeGaulle Hotel, on Pembroke near the Strand, was undergoing general interior renovations. It was still better than the best in Moscow.

When I arrived, the temporary front desk had a reservation for me. They had a letter, too. The billing was made out to the Angos Shipping Lines, S.A., Athens. "Do you mind staying on the fourth floor above the construction," asked the clerk? "The room is only just redone, and the workmen on the third won't bother you at night. In fact, you will be the only one up there until the Scottish football team arrives next week."

Did I care? About construction, about privacy - no, I wanted privacy! I pulled open the door to the small elevator and rode to the fourth floor, listening to the mechanical click and whir as I was lifted. I again opened the old-style elevator door, this time needing a little stronger push. It was slightly stuck. I walked down the hall to my room door.

Indeed, the floor did seem to have been just redone. The paint smelled so fresh, I touched the wall to see if it was wet. It was barely dry. After Moscow's dull colors, the forest green hall was pleasant. The new, thick brown rug made a dull sound, as though I was walking on sand as I moved across it.

In my "new" room, I opened the letter from the

desk to find £5,000 and another, slightly used Canadian passport courtesy of my Russian benefactors. I lay down on the bed, fully dressed, after tying the briefcase to my left arm with the cord from the hotel laundry bag. I drifted to sleep thinking that I would have loved to have had a good stiff drink. Two stiff drinks. Anything but Vodka.

Next morning, I left the DeGaulle, bought new clothes at a small shop on Guards Street, returned and waited. At the end of the first day, it occurred to me that I was no longer in Moscow and the walls did not have eyes or ears. Dressed for business, briefcase in hand, I began taking cabs around London for short hops, occasionally walking into and out of Tube entrances.

I felt I could spot Russians, but back then, the Soviets used East Germans in Western Europe because they blended in better. I knew I'd have a hard time figuring out if anyone was following me, even though some of my training had been devoted to the intelligence arts. I desperately wanted to open the case and see the contents, almost expecting the case to explode, burn - who could tell? In the back of one cab, I held my breath and pressed the catch button, causing the spring to push open.

Nothing happened.

I looked inside - all I saw was a box of Red Star Typing Paper, the linen finish, watermarked paper used in higher, official circles. It had three rubber bands around it. The box had been used before, evidenced by it's frayed edges.

I removed it from the briefcase. It felt heavy, as though filled with paper. It was packed, almost bowing the top. I don't know why, but I sniffed it. I smelled solvent, fresh plastic, and the musty paper of the box.

I took another cab, then another, then checked into a cheap hotel in the East End. The Sumatra. I didn't care about the room, so much as the privacy. The clerk didn't care about me so much as the tenners I tossed on the counter.

Once in the room, I took off my coat, sat on the bed, and opened the case. I took out the paper box, removed the rubber bands, and took off the top.

The contents were paper, many pieces of yellowed, old paper, wrapped in clouded plastic. The wrapping was sealed with a plastic card that had been chemically glued to the bag's plastic. The card had a hologram of a red star on it that moved when I shifted the package to peer inside. I could not open the package without tearing the plastic, and I could not remove the card without braking the seal. I held the package in my hands, removed the cover from the incandescent bedside lamp for more light, and tried to see inside the wrapping.

Then I realized my fingerprints were all over the box, the plastic and the card! What if the box had been sealed with matching line marks that I failed to realign when I put things back? What if the plastic had been "clean" when I touched it. What an idiot I'd been! I felt like a schoolboy trying to sneak a copy of an upcoming exam without leaving a trace; but this headmaster would kill me if I was discovered. I felt like a drowning man, desperately trying to swim in deep, fast currents.

I dressed, went downstairs, walked across the street to a small, dimly lit pub and began to drink. At first I was afraid, then indifferent. After a large quantity of cold lager and Scotch whiskey, I felt the fool's courage that floods out of the bottle to brace foundering men when all else is failing. The briefcase was at my feet as I sat on a stool at the bar. I stood up, a bit shakily, and moved into the dining area. As soon as I sat down, I ordered a light fish meal and more beer. Outside, London rain had begun, getting quite heavy. Water started to run in the gutter across the street, carrying odd bits of newspaper and an empty can. A giant rat dashed out in the rain from behind a car parked in front of the Sumatra, looked up and down the roadway, then ran back to cover.

I pulled open the case and removed the paper box. I looked at it for several seconds. Then my hands acted on their own. I watched as though they were independent of me, like viewing a film. The rubber bands came off. One tore. I opened the box. The plastic bag came out. I ripped the card carefully from the plastic, to be met by an oddly pleasant odor, a hint of spice and confined paper, from the pages inside.

I folded the plastic back slowly, like unpeeling tight wrapping on a fragile gift.

No scientific doodles or computer sheets. It was handwriting on old paper, collected and preserved in this condition, perhaps even in this box, for years. No, I thought, hologram seals are new. This was put together for delivery.

I ate. The food was surprisingly excellent. I drank. The liquor was local bootleg in brand-name bottles, but not bad. I studied the papers in a light stupor.

Suddenly, I became uncomfortably sober.

The Cyrillic alphabet is fairly simple. Old Russian handwriting is easier to read than old French or English script. The language itself has changed little in one thousand years.

It is difficult, however, to read Russian handwriting when the author is not a native writer, or when the author is very old or ill. Russian script is highly functional, but not very distinctive by flourish or calligraphic art. I recalled that Lenin's script had deteriorated badly as he matured. He was a prodigious reader, writer and note taker, but had terrible penmanship after 1920.

I sifted through the papers until I found a clear page, preserved in the middle of the pile. It had been folded over. The writing was black, made with a fountain pen. The paper was brown, thick, used for wrapping. One edge was smooth; three were jagged, as though torn from a larger sheet.

I could read it. It was a kind of diary page, a private memorandum, full of idiom, insult and either incorrect or playful syntax.

It had a scrawled signature at an angle on the bottom of the page. "Koba."

With that, I searched the pile and found a few more "Kobas" which reinforced my interest and fear.

If the Fifth Directorate man was telling me the truth, then there was no copy of this material left in the Soviet Union. It's existence was heretofore unknown to me. What would Rome want with this pile of 35 year old paper? What secrets could have been so dire that they needed clandestine transport under threat of death.

The papers were notes, evidently in the handwriting of one "Koba." Koba was the nickname of Joseph Djugashvili, a man born in 1879 in the town of Gori, in Tsarist Georgia who later acquired a shorter name before the Bolshevik revolution in 1917.

Joseph Stalin.

I paid my bill, packed the papers and returned, across the street, to the privacy of the Sumatra. I studied through the night, experiencing heights of astonishment, one after the other.

The papers, if genuine, were sensational. They were the reflections of a man afraid of dying, covering much of his life in fragmented pieces of memory, written, from the condition and type of paper used, as the mood came and went.

The more I read, the more I could see why the Soviets would not keep copies around. Why not destroy them? Bureaucrats save paper for two reasons: habit and power.

These pages had power.

You have heard the rumors about Lenin's lost second political testament? It may never have existed. Occasional scholars believe it did, but that it was destroyed by the Politburo or by Stalin himself upon Lenin's death in January, 1924. Was I holding Stalin's lost political testament?

I read all the next day, working on translations, mentally reviewing the consistency and flow of what I was reading, becoming convinced that I was holding either genuine papers or a wild attempt at forgery for a grand political result I could not readily understand.

Toward evening my tired eyes hurt. I had read and re-read all the papers. Many were read a third time. I rearranged their order, first by dates, then according to the type of paper used. I next arranged them by the size of the paper, then tried to put them in order of handwriting deterioration. There was no consistency, only a progression of illegibility in penmanship. Many final pages had dates; just as many did not. "Koba" appeared on twenty different entries, but was absent from most. I believe the same hand wrote all the materials, but the penmanship varied beyond the norms of morning/nighttime or moving/stationary. The author was probably sick, losing control of his ability to write.

According to the texts, he expected to be murdered. That wasn't all: Lenin had died as a result of foul play!

Who was the priest coming to take this from me? Where was the material going? My brain ached. My eyes felt scratchy from irregular sleep and the roller coaster of alcohol. Was I beginning to go mad from imaginary tension or was it too real?

I didn't know - couldn't know, because so much had happened so fast all around me, I couldn't catch up. I was doubled, you see.

I had been sent to hide within their house, yet they knew about my mission the whole time. All I had seen and done for several years was a lie. I lied to them and they lied to me in order to lie to my superiors.

If the KGB knew about me when I left, they knew about me when I went in. I had wasted that time. What mattered was a case of papers. Was it more of the lie? Was I a fool of such magnitude? Worse, was I a fool again, for a second time?

I lay back on the stiff bed, on a light-brown spread that had carried the tired weight of many travellers. I felt my heart palpitate, fighting the tension I was producing all on my own. I listened to myself panic in that same, fast water, way over my head. I was drowning. Minutes of internal torture passed.

Then I turned.

I pushed my concern aside. I saw the limit of my

control, of my courage, and smashed through with pent up energy and anger, the way an athlete overcomes pain.

I had the papers. Someone wanted them. No more games, I thought. No more fool. I pictured the extreme of possible pain and humiliation and found I could fight through.

If it was beyond me, then it was God's will. It was not my burden alone. I had made myself a character from the works of Dostoyevsky: strong, thoughtful, but unable to make a decision. Thought without action is torment. It cuts down the jumping champion in midair by killing the desire to win. It crushes the will better than external repression.

I tore off the bonds and grabbed back my determination, flushing out my fears with the raw, hot power of anger. In the moment I conquered my limits, I knew what I had to do.

I left the Sumatra for confrontation at the De-Gaulle. I would know. I would finally know. Two days had passed. The time had come.

I took the Tube back, walking from the station with ready anticipation. I had been away for some time, violating my instructions. When I arrived at the hotel desk, I retrieved my key from the young woman working as the night clerk. She bade me a good night. The wall clock showed slightly after midnight. Her little radio was tuned to BBC classical through the night.

I knew there were few other guests in the hotel because I hadn't seen many in the lobby and most room keys hung from their hooks, at the desk. But for me, my floor was empty. As the small elevator door opened, I thought about the three men in the gray

Ford Escort down the street from the hotel entrance. I knew.

Only Russians would pretend to read a newspaper in a car in the dark as I passed by on the street. The elevator rose to my floor, the fourth. I got out. There were six floors in total.

I took the stair to the flat roof and left the priceless papers in the glow of the full moon, placing the briefcase against a vent pipe. Either they were beyond value or they truly had no value as forgeries. I went down the stair again, but left the top, roof door pushed open. As I went down, I removed the light bulbs from each fixture down to the main level. Only the red basement "Exit" light filtered up. I took the fire axe from the second floor landing. The glass casing opened easily, without sound. The axe had a red, painted metal head, the very color of blood. The wooden handle was smooth and cool. It had never been used.

As I re-climbed the stairs, I wondered how old the axe was. Who had put it on the rack I had taken it from? Had anyone ever thought it might be used to save a life in such an odd manner?

I walked up to the fourth floor. I spat on the door hinges and worked them back and forth to make sure they were silent. I took a £5 note from my wallet, folded it and placed it on the striker plate as I gently closed the door, stopping the latch mechanism from engaging.

I took off my shoes, and waited.

My eyes got used to the gentle light from above and the red, low wattage light from the basement, below. Brighter hallway light leaked around the outline of the stair door. The lobby was silent except for the little radio at the desk playing Bach, then Mozart, then Handel in full length, concert performance. Two hours passed. It was not unpleasant, waiting there. If I was tired before, I was ready now. I sat on the stairs. My eyes and ears were keenly attentive.

I heard the front door of the DeGaulle open. I think I heard the elevator button pushed - perhaps I imagined it; but I heard the elevator move, each sound of the gears, linkage and cable giving me energy.

Would they go to the fifth floor and walk down one as they should, or would they be careless because they were dealing with only a priest? I trusted them to be confident. They came to kill in numbers and with purpose.

The elevator stopped at four, right beside me. They opened the door. Without talking, I heard them moving. I saw their shadows pass in front of the stair door, momentarily blocking the light around the door outline. I heard one stop after taking a few steps. Two proceeded down the hall. The door to my room was about 25 paces away. I heard them move the distance on the thick carpet, then stop. They were listening for me as I listened to them.

My heart began to race, getting ready. I heard the one closest to the door take a deep breath, signalling action. I knew the other two would be moving.

I silently opened the stairwell door with my left hand as the axe head rested on my right shoulder, the handle strongly gripped in my right hand. It happened fast.

They had pistols with "long necks" as the Latinos call silencers in the bush. The closest one began to turn, sensing me behind him in spite of the action starting down the hall.

Before I saw his face, as I was bringing the fire axe down to split his head apart, I caught the scent of the cologne again.

In the same moment he saw me, as he was bringing the pistol up, toward me, as the Russians were kicking through my hotel door to kill me and take the papers, I smashed the axe into the top of Bishop D'Albret's head with all my weight and might, sending the steel right down to his jaw.

As D'Albret fell over, dying, the Russians had just burst into my room, thinking their rear protected. I heard the "thud, thud" sound of fists smashing into a weight bag. They were shooting the place up before looking under the bed, in the bathroom or the small closet. I picked up D'Albret's pistol and walked down the hall. I looked in the door as both Russians turned to leave the room.

Maybe it was the blood all over me, maybe it was the weapon levelled at their faces. They both went wide-eyed and stiff with surprise. The younger, bigger one began to back up in fear. The braver, perhaps more experienced one with the moustache went to raise his weapon.

I shot him right through his moustache.

As his head was snapping back, I shot the other in the left eye. When both were down, I shot each several times more to keep them down. It was 2:30 AM.

I collected their Walther P-38 pistols and put them on the bed. I pushed the dead men against the far wall.

I walked back down the hall, pulled the axe from D'Albret's head and dragged him down to my room, leaving a dark trail in the brown rug. I walked to the stairwell and retrieved my shoes.

The loudest noise had been the kick the Russians gave the door, breaking the jamb apart at the lock. Their falling bodies had been the next most disturbing. I closed the door against the broken frame as lightly as possible, after removing little pieces of splintered wood from the rug in front of my door. Once the rug was cleaned, and the door closed, I sat on the bed to catch my breath.

Nothing. No one came. No one had heard.

I looked at the three of them. Who were they, really? Was D'Albret one of the famous Russian boyos who are found after long years of intelligence work, buried like termites in the fabric of society, of religious or political organizations?

The young muscle was in his late twenties. The older Russian was about forty-five. His face was deeply lined from years of sun and exposure, quite different from the Moscow paleness I was used to. He was tall, about 6 feet. The younger one was taller still and heavier. Either could have killed me bare handed. Either would have.

And D'Albret - what kind of bishop carried a weapon? I had seen Russians before in Latin America. As soon as they settled in as military or intelligence advisors, they act like cowboys and carry Walther pistols, perhaps because they hate the Germans so much. I often wondered why American soldiers developed an affection for the AK-47 rifle.

I sat looking at the first men I had ever killed. I felt tired, but alive. I was soaked with sweat. Still no one came. I took a very fast shower, washing D'Albret's blood from my face and hands. I changed my clothes, leaving the bloody ones on the bed.

And I went to leave. I had clothes on my back,

money in my pocket and valuable papers on the roof.
Three men had died for them. It was 2:50 AM.

I went to open the door, but it was lightly stuck,
despite my prior, careful closing. I had to jerk it open.
I looked down the hall before leaving. Clear.

Then I looked down at the brown rug by my feet
and saw something that had not been there before.

A chewed, wooden match with a yellow sulphur
tip.

Then I knew.

Oh yes, the papers were real. If I didn't know who
D'Albret really was, I knew who he worked for.

I went to the telephone book and looked up their
number. I called their embassy and, in my best Moscow accent, briefly told the duty officer that some of
their trash had turned up in my room and they should
come and get it before I called the London authorities.

The embassy operator told me he had no idea
what I meant and cut me off. I didn't tell him where
I was - didn't have to. I imagined I could see the
operator cutting the connection, jumping up and
running to the KGB resident's door, knocking to rouse
the sleeping official and disclose the call.

At the same time the telephone tappers at Scotland Yard, Special Branch would be doing the identical
drill, rousing their people. If a car left the embassy, the
Yard would be right behind it. The embassy would
send a crew to clean up. "Let them," I thought.

I left the room, and went to the roof to get the
papers. As I bent over to pick them up, a voice made
me stop in mid-motion.

"He organized it, you know. We didn't want the
Pope shot, but those people in the Fourth Directorate
are not controllable. He was going to do it again. But

Fifth Directorate didn't know which one he was. He wasn't ours. We had to find him and stop him. They have had him there for years. We heard of him indirectly."

I stood and looked at him. He was matter-of-fact about the recent events. He continued," Yes, the papers are genuine. Take them. Keep them, but, mind you, keep them safe."

"Why are you letting me go," I asked him?

He stepped closer to me, closer that we could look into each other's eyes and touch each other's minds. "They have people in my Directorate. I have mine in theirs. I am not letting you go anywhere. They will come for you again. They must. He was not the only one. I think there are two more in Rome. He was the only active one, for now. There will be another."

"They know what you have. They know you will use it if anything happens to the Pope."

He cut me off before I could ask him, sensing my question, "There are things that must happen to my country. You'll see. But, if they kill the Pope, nothing will happen - maybe a war will happen. They are there, in the Vatican. If I knew who, I would tell you. You were supposed to be a courier to the direct agent of the Pope. They knew you were coming and what you were bringing. They had to stop you. If you had not killed him, I would have."

"You cannot trust any of the people in Rome, unless you know for sure. If you give those papers away to the wrong ones, they'll try to kill the Pope again. They want the trouble it will cause. Keep the papers. Disappear. They will not act if you hold Moscow's exposure in your hands. Disappear, my friend, where even I can't find you."

"For how long," I demanded?

"Until things change. Until they have lost their power. Until they don't matter anymore. Maybe a year, maybe forever. You'll know when the world has changed and the papers don't seem as powerful because the secrets are known and the walls have come down. The Pope will be safe then."

He must have sensed my disbelief. I had only just been in Moscow. "Yes," he instructed me with his longer experience, "you may see change."

"Where should I go? How can I hide from them?"

This time, he bent over, picked up the case and put it in my hands, as he had three days ago, far away. He put one arm around me and directed me to the stair. He walked with me. "Yes, we are everywhere. We are in the universities, the churches, the political parties, the unions, the police, the businesses. We are thousands and we see and hear through thousands more. We hear all the West. I could find you anywhere in the West, even on the North Pole. So can the Fourth Directorate."

"But I have an idea," he said.

We left the Hotel DeGaulle together and walked for two blocks, then around a corner. A gray Ford shot by at high speed. Five seconds later a black Toyota van followed. Next, three cabs followed, each filled with burly passengers in raincoats.

"Exactly how good is your German," he asked me in a rich beer hall accent from Munich.

From that day until recently, while pretending I was of German extraction, I've lived in a small town, Raz, in northwest Romania, an area populated by ethnic Hungarians and Germans. I worked in the province offices, appraising and collecting taxes on personal property. Everyone hated me. No one would talk to me. The Germans hated me as a traitor to German traditions. The Hungarians hate the Germans on principle and the Romanians hate everybody, especially tax collectors. Fifth Directorate dropped me there. I stayed. Fourth Directorate scoured the West, looking for me.

I never learned my benefactor's real name.

One day, last December, I saw a picture of a boisterous meeting of the Soviet Parliament, where the first uncontrolled political debate since the Kerensky Duma was heard in official Moscow.

The world was shaking. The Communist system was dying. It was cracking and could not be repaired. I studied the picture in the week-old copy of Izvestia very closely. He looked older, although news photos have a way of making men look older and fatter. I wondered if he still chewed matches.

And I knew it was time to leave.

Eventually, I went with the first wave of refugees to hit Austria when Romania fell. With no dependents and my western currency, I could move quickly.

I went first to Canada, to Newfoundland where whole nations could hide for a short time from daylight itself or the prying eyes of searchers. I left, came south, and arrived here. I would have stayed in Canada, but he was wrong.

True, the political conditions have changed and the Pope is safe, but Fourth Directorate is not after me for that. Russians simply hold grudges.

They feast on history as their present bread. They live passions from beyond the memory of living men. They mean to find me because I killed three of them. That chase will never end, even if they become raving capitalists. They take their own vows that go beyond politics.

But, I cannot live in confinement forever. I faced them once. I will again. And again, if I must.

These papers have lost their original importance. They no longer secure a balance for the Pope's life.

Stalin has been exposed. Their entire system has been exposed. The atrocities have been admitted. Take these papers, old friend. Show them to the world so that their existence is known for all generations, in case another oppression like theirs might arise."

MY STORY IN MY WORDS

I looked at FX.

My heart had travelled far in life, thrilling to challenge, fighting despair, yet his story moved me in a new way. He had turned to fight an adversary that had the power to regenerate, capable of sending wave after wave of assassins after him.

"Come with me," I urged him. "I have friends that can hide you. They can help you."

"Padraig," he sighed in the drizzle, "I've been hiding. The time is now. I won't hide any longer." He paused, looking at me. "Do you understand?"

I did.

I wanted to protect him, to meet the challenge at his side, walking, if need be into a gun fight that very night. But, he was right. Logic demanded that the papers be safeguarded immediately. By me.

"They" would come for him, no matter what politics were in Moscow. It's the way of the world. He had been marked for death ever since the Fifth Direc-orate had sent him out with the papers. He was also right that they were everywhere. If not today, they would come tomorrow.

"Here, take these damn papers." He put the case under my legs as we sat. I accepted them. Their political power was gone, like a bomb defused. The conflict was not political any longer. It was men in pursuit of a man.

"Goodbye," he said as he reached for my hand. I took it. There was nothing I could do. I held his hand in a parting grip. I stood up. "Adios, pal," I said.

I held the case and walked in the direction of my office. Half a block away I turned, looking back. He was walking down Sixteenth in the direction of the Soviet Embassy, toward the White House. I thought, by reflex, of left hand, right hand, get dead first, walk, shoot. I wanted to trail behind and back him when he touched the fire. But he was right.

I turned, walking slowly to my office, my heart grown tender. Several minutes passed.

Then I heard the distant "wump, wump" sound that a short barrel pump shotgun makes on a deserted city street when two shots are fired in fast succession. I stopped for a moment, looking down. A single pistol report echoed.

I walked on. No sirens.

In the services, there is a tradition of sending messages. Soldiers are not politicians, not in the field. The generals become politicians when they become fat and lazy, at home. At times, soldiers speak clearly to say a matter is ended. Politicians can't.

I called a friend of mine, a retired Marine Colonel, the next day and asked if the night shift had found anyone. "Meet me for lunch," he said.

We met for a lunchtime stroll in the National

Gallery of Art. He was a trifle late as he rushed to greet me at the main entrance.

I asked for some detail. We walked down the main hall to the east wing. As we entered the beautiful courtyard garden, he told me they had found a man dumped on the small quad behind the Jackson Statue in Lafayette Park, right by the White House. Mobile telephone call. No ready identification. Shotgunned.

"Did he get off a round," I asked quietly, seeking a measure of revenge for my dead friend.

He looked at me with a slight surprise. Then he relaxed. I noticed a wrinkle of pain in his eyes as he spoke, "not unless a Meerlug can fire."

I couldn't respond.

I sat on a bench, listening to water trickle in the lovely, sculpted fountain only a few feet away. I studied geometric lines in the gray marble floor, noticing natural faults in the glossed finish. The air felt bone cold. My hands rested, limp, in my lap.

"After you called," he softly assured me, "I made a few inquiries. I drove over to Langley - just got back. Your family name is in this." I looked up.

He handed me a small pocket bible, back from travel through avenues of adventure. Indeed, my friend had been well armed.

My Marine left me to a private moment.

I read.

****

This book, while my translation, is a Jesuit's work. I expect he proceeds in good stead as a champion who honored his fourth vow unto finality.

Pax vobiscum, FX.

CHAPTER TWO

TRANSLATION METHOD

It has been three months since I left FX on a dark night. The present urgency of the translations has occupied me so that I have not had time to dwell on past events. While I have labored under a promise, I have pushed, at speed, under my own compulsion.

At first, I tried working alone, moving aside my schedule with the generous help of colleagues who assumed my cases. While I am quite capable in everyday Russian and German, FX was right: the handwriting and use of idioms was a severe problem for any but the most accomplished linguist and historian.

I contacted old acquaintances in the most general way, using a story that has floated around for years: that a copy of Lenin's secret diary was available from a secure source at a high price, and that I needed help to determine if it was real. According to the "classic" story, bona-fide experts are not initially allowed to review the proffered document in each offering. It's always a fraud. Intermediaries such as myself, familiar with deals, but without document expertise, can examine the papers. Then, a "good faith" down payment is usually required before an expert is allowed to study the material under the most controlled and negotiated circumstances. These negotiations can go on for days. Of course, before any examination, the down payment disappears, along with the seller. A scam.

There are conning masters who regularly travel the world peddling Lenin's diary to gullible moguls. Such "deals of a lifetime" are made several times a year. The last price I heard mentioned was 40 million dollars. The down payment to show good faith was $650,000. The artist was the Italian Professor Ponaccio. And the dupe - his third Japanese collector in two years. The prices have surprisingly escalated, now that the Soviet Union is in danger of disappearing in favor of a centralized slavic state, built around the Ukraine and Greater Russia.

Because of these constant Lenin scams, it is not difficult to find experts on Russian handwriting. However, very few are familiar with Stalin, because he was not the prolific writer Lenin was. Lenin was always writing, speaking or getting ready to write.

I eventually spent almost an entire month in Finland with Rik Kerbüssøn, one of the dependable Lenin scholars.

It was still winter in the far north. I knew he had done occasional work for NATO, and for very private intelligence groups scattered throughout the West. I had indirectly searched him out through English contacts from an earlier acquisition. I had been involved with a deal to acquire the secret diary of Inessa

Armand, the only woman Lenin may have passionately loved. The deal fell. No documents were produced; no deposit made.

As far as I know, the seller, allegedly an aged Wermacht Officer who spent World War Two on embassy duty in Switzerland, was legitimate. He pulled away for unexplained reasons, returning to Lucerne, making me suspicious that he was an agent for an undisclosed principal who wanted to test the market - probably before stealing the genuine diary from whoever possessed it. Valuable documents exist in a very private, very illegal market.

Great delicacy is required to obtain document experts, yet keep the deal confidential. Many of these documents might impact existing governments. Attracting the attention of thieves is the least of one's worries. As an example, there is virtually no market for documents attributable to Mao Ze Dong (modern spelling) because the Long Marchers who remain in power in Bejing will send agents to either buy the material at a ridiculously low price or take it back by any means possible, including murder. No informed collector will touch Mao originals.

Kerbüssøn was known for discretion, unmatched gifts in the slavic languages, and an excellent historical background in the development of the Soviet Union from the October Revolution to the present. He had also spent time in a gulag after an innocent trip to see relatives in the Soviet Union in 1958. He hated Russian Communists with a special passion because he was one quarter Russian.

He was still a strapping figure, standing 6"4" and, if thinner, still moved like the cross-country skiing champion he had been. He left an eye behind in the gulag and wore a patch these days. Like many Scandinavians, he was addicted to pipe smoking, saunas and eating heavily salted sardines. He had thick, white hair and blazing blue eyes, full of life. His wife, Sonja Bekar, the famous Finnish artist, had been dead seven years.

When I met him in his cramped "Import-Export" offices in the small Rensar Building in old Helsinki, I tried the "Lenin Diary" story to get background without showing him any of my real documents. He thought it over, but told me to go elsewhere, referring me to Professor Spikov at Oxford or Professor Roboshilov at Georgetown, back in Washington, DC. I knew these two, but wanted to enlist the best.

I tried to persuade him that each of those gentlemen was not proven secure, but he continued to insist he wasn't interested.

In Lenin.

I took him to dinner one night at the Hotel Rialto, overlooking the working harbor. It's a small, private room featuring the best of Finnish cuisine: simply prepared fish. We first had a general conversation, but finally got down to business. Small fishing boats were coming in for the day from the frigid dark, hard working sailors struggling as they have been throughout history, to extract their living from the cruel Baltic Sea. I told Kerbüssøn that my first story was not quite true. He was hardly surprised, and shrugged while continuing to eat kipper appetizers with raw onion. He drank Dutch beer. When he asked the suspected origin, I said only, "Soso."

He mind came to alert attention. He understood immediately. "Soso," is the colloquial equivalent of "Joey," in Georgian. It was Stalin's nickname as a young boy.

Rik was hooked.

Very little original Stalin material is available because Stalin was so secretive. What may have existed was probably destroyed either by Stalin when he was alive or by Malenkov and Khrushchev immediately after Stalin's death. The bulk of Stalin's published works were ghosted by other hack writers.

Stalin was sensitive about his accented Russian. He had no political motive to compile a diary legacy. Lenin, on the other hand, lived politics. Stalin executed politicians. He detested them. If anything, Stalin was an amateur historian, impressed by achievements, not intellectual discussions.

I made a deal with Rik.

I wouldn't let him see the actual papers. He would teach me to decipher the handwriting based on occasional samples and daily study of the Kerbüssøn method. He was expert on idioms, names and peculiar Bolshevik uses of ordinary words. I agreed at first that he could have a copy of the materials 1 year later, but could not have the originals. Later, he changed this condition as a point of honor.

He wasn't interested in money for this job - he would have paid me for the opportunity. Yet, I have taken excellent care of his Zurich bank account.

We worked at his small summer home in Malk, about 40 kilometers outside Helsinki. He left word with his part time male secretary, Mickie, that he had gone skiing for the month, a very common occurrence in Finland where workers are more notorious than in Germany for taking unscheduled, long, sports vacations. I spent an exhausting month working 18 hours a day, every day with him. While I matched his enthusiasm, I did not have his physical stamina. He was just over 70 years old and still liked to finish the day with a few large belts of 100 proof Finnish table Vodka, a potential alternative fuel for automobiles and nuclear reactors.

We lived a hectic life, working in the single large room heated by an ancient iron stove that burned wood and coal. We melted snow for water, and ate canned food, except for the deer he shot early one morning as I slept, exhausted, and the fish he caught through a hole in the ice on the frozen pond, while I worked.

He loved the outdoors. I didn't.

But, I learned my desired lessons. He gave me special insight. He force fed me mountains of other-wise undocumented knowledge and helped me beyond what I can ever repay. Once I told him about my meeting with FX, he abruptly insisted on never seeing the documents in their entirety, because he felt it was not his privilege - it was mine. He also didn't want the responsibility, which was mine, alone.

He told me I should never release the originals because they would ultimately disappear into the black market, becoming mixed with the vulgarity of cash and delivery. If a man had died for the papers, they should be kept separate from the currency of collector avarice. Thieves will take documents like these and destroy them. Then, they will travel the world selling "origi-nals," to various dupes.

My work uses the Kerbüssøn method. Whereas he would translate to modern English, I have translated to modern American. The originals are in a special vault in Utah, secure in the protection of people who can be trusted in any matters concerning the Soviets.

But understand, I have not attempted to provide a literal translation for scholars because the utility of such work is limited to academic audiences. Long after Marxism and militant Scientific Socialism are dead in practical politics, their evil will linger on in the cultural entente of Socialist academia.

Marxism is a complex, artificial subject. It can motivate the most circular, unending debates, the stuff of scholarly monographs no one reads. It has and will continue to serve as the angst apologia of the sons and daughters of privilege who "study" its meaning in great western universities while enjoying full stomachs, medical insurance and automobiles - commodities unknown to most men, except in their dreams.

The rest of the world knows the real Marx. The hard experience of humanity has been declared in bloody revolt, smashed barriers and soon, hopefully, the cremation of Lenin's body.

I have worked from Russian and German. The papers are primarily in Russian, but Stalin was fluent in both. His first language was Georgian. He never wrote in Georgian in surviving political papers.

Georgians who speak Russian sound like Italians speaking English. Georgian has a musical quality and the phonetic sounds blend together. Russian, like German, is guttural. Each word can be distinguished from the next. A Russian speaking French sounds like a slipping transmission, unwieldy and uneven.

Russian, however, is a powerful language for public speaking. It sounds clear when shouted.

My translation will not be accurate in fifty years, as our own Americanized English changes. In fifty years, the original papers will be available, and other scholars, this time true historians, can hammer it out.

By then, Soso's ideas may have been reapplied in politics. They are being used to some extent in business methods in the United States today, in accord with the Generalissimo's prediction.

There are ideas too dangerous for ordinary usage, lest their context be forgotten, and their danger ignored.

Kerbüssøn warned me to take a special care for myself. He called it "the presence."

Scholars can become immersed in research, so that they live in the past, unable to accommodate the present. It occurs little by little, gathering momentum until the victim is lost in the dialogue of a dead generation. He told me to be cautious while he checked on an old rumor about a missing Stalin relative that might add background. That was news to me. He said it was remote, something he had heard in the madness of the gulag. Probably rubbish. Maybe he didn't hear it. He wished me Godspeed.

He also gave me one of the famous miniatures painted by his wife. I had complimented her touch in the piece entitled "Blue on Blue." I am looking at it as I write these words, wondering if I should put this chapter in the book for fear of exposing Rik to any danger from the Soviets or from the West for working free lance. My concern is real.

At the same moment, I can feel the cold from the Malk forest, the drizzle on Scott Circle and the passion of sworn obligation.

"The purpose of enduring, meaningful art," an accomplished master once told me, "is to make you feel alive!"

What you do after that depends on your interpretation. And desire.

CHAPTER THREE

SHORT BIOGRAPHY

None of what we "know" about Joseph Stalin should be taken as absolute fact.

He was born in an area where the Church kept the best records. Notice I did not say accurate - just the comparative "best." Two major wars disrupted people and places throughout Europe and Russia. The Soviets had an interesting habit of doctoring photos and historical facts to suit the cause of the Revolution.

Truth did not matter; the Revolution mattered. Stalin, personally, was an excellent propagandist.

When in supreme power after 1929, he was often involved in the arts as the final censor. He was exceptionally literate. Stalin was fluent in three languages, Georgian, Russian, and German. He studied Latin and Greek in his seminary years.

He could read and write French and English. All the Old Bolsheviks, the movers and shakers of the original Revolution, were internationalists because they had to be - they lived through internal and then foreign exile all over Europe.

Don't be impressed with the breath of Stalin's linguistic achievements. I once met a train conductor in Italy who spoke six languages. I counted them as he worked his way through my compartment and the hall along the train car, packed with holiday revelers headed for the Riviera.

Stalin's favorite films were American Westerns. He used to play several in a row in his private theater, keeping cronies up, drinking hard liquor all night. He enjoyed reading the works of the German Author, Thomas Mann. He studied the American Constitution and Declaration of Independence thoroughly before he personally wrote the revised Soviet Constitution in 1936.

Who was Stalin?

He was born as Joseph Vissarionovich Djugashvili on December 21, 1879, in the rural Georgian town of Gori. His mother was Ekaterina; his father Vissarion. Vissarion was a drunk. He beat Joseph on a regular basis. Eventually, Vissarion deserted the family. Ekaterina raised Joseph by doing wash, cleaning - anything. They were extremely poor. This is not a picturesque description. They lived in abject squalor, far below the norm for Gori, barely struggling along.

Stalin's left arm was lame and about three inches shorter than his right. The reason: unknown. It could have been from birth or childhood injury.

Despite his poverty, he was an excellent student. He eventually won a scholarship to the local Russian Orthodox seminary at Tiflis, which was the capital of Georgia at the time. This was a significant achievement for an abused, poverty-stricken child. The Church was one of the pinnacles of Russian society.

Georgians profess in the Greek Orthodox Church. Stalin received his scholarship training in the Russian Orthodox Church, which promised the possibility of a good life under the Tsar's sponsorship.

If he entered the Russian Orthodox Church as a cleric, he would be part of the elite. What did he do? He studied Marx and turned into a revolutionary. In 1899 he was tossed out of the seminary.

At 19, after four years in the seminary, he was off and running into Red history.

He went into the socialist underground in Georgia, trying to raise hell by organizing demonstrations to goad the Tsar's officers into committing acts of violent repression. He was so wild, the Georgian Socialists gave him the boot.

In 1902 he was in the oil fields of Baku, organizing strikes. He was arrested, kept in jail for a while and sent off to his first exile in Siberia. He returned in 1904.

Lenin was writing political pamphlets to stir the Russian populace at this time. The famous Socialist conference, the one the modern Soviets hearken back to, took place in London in 1903. Lenin's group wanted a small, tightly controlled Revolutionary elite. Power would be concentrated at the top and would remain there. The masses would be led - from the very top. No disagreement would be tolerated.

The conference vote approved this. The word "Bolshevik" means majority. The minority, the "Mensheviks," were more democratically inclined. Lenin never disguised his ambition or the fact that he meant to be ruthless, keeping power absolutely in the hands of the top few leaders. When Stalin returned from Siberia in 1904, he fell in with the Lenin-led Bolsheviks.

Stalin was young, single and literate. He attached himself to Lenin like a shadow.

The Bolsheviks were in regular financial trouble. Stalin organized bank robberies to raise cash for the

Bolsheviks. He paid his intellectual dues by travelling into Russia to incite political troubles, getting caught and being resentenced to several exiles.

He didn't serve in the Russian Army in World War One because of his useless left arm. When the Tsar abdicated the throne in 1917 after the army moved against him, Stalin was again in exile in Siberia.

Stalin fought wolves, braved deadly temperatures and storms, and nearly died from exposure in the harsh Siberian environs. He was a physically tough man, despite the handicap of a useless arm and his small stature - 5 feet 5 inches.

He left exile and returned to Petrograd. The Tsar was replaced by the Socialist Kerensky government. The Bolsheviks shortly replaced the indecisive Kerensky by force.

Lenin was in power after the October Bolshevik coup in 1917. The Bolsheviks pulled Russia out of the war, as promised, by surrender to the Germans with huge concessions of territory in Poland and the Ukraine. The Bolsheviks then fought an intense, bloody civil war with political adversaries. Few prisoners were taken. The Bolsheviks, by 1920 had won against the odds.

Then, they tried to take Poland and were savagely defeated.

Next, in 1921, a terrible famine came. The Bolsheviks tried to keep it secret, but it got so bad they finally accepted foreign aid. Millions starved to death all through the empire, even in Moscow.

The traditional capital of Russia was St. Petersburg, or Petrograd, but that city was too exposed to foreign (German) invasion, so the Bolsheviks moved the capital back into the heartland - Moscow, which was the ancient capital.

Fanny Kaplan shot Lenin several times in an assassination attempt in 1918, but he survived, carrying a bullet in his body for the remainder of his life. He recovered completely.

In mid-1922, Lenin had his first stroke. Ultimately, there would be no survival. Lenin's father had died of a stroke in his middle age. In December, 1922, Lenin had another stroke. He became physically debilitated for several months then began to recover. He had another stroke in April, 1923. He could not speak clearly, write, or command. He had a final stroke in January, 1924 and died that month.

The only significant military adventure involving Stalin was the disastrous Polish campaign in 1921. Stalin took care of "the books" thereafter in the relatively minor post of Party Secretary.

He was a bureaucrat. The Politburo sent him off on a few missions in the field, but he was given rather boring work.

As Secretary, he posted his cronies throughout the growing Soviet Government. While Trotsky was out winning the Civil War as Commander of the Red Army, Stalin was busy taking over the back room by placing people and offering rewards for fidelity - to him. He served briefly as the Commissar or Commissioner for Nationalities.

When Lenin died, no clear successor was in sight. Lenin had never appointed a political heir. Stalin had fallen from Lenin's favor because of Stalin's blunt methods of accumulating power.

The assumption was that Lenin would be succeeded by Trotsky. Stalin won out by cunning and action at the right time.

By 1929, Trotsky was kicked out of the Soviet Union. He was murdered in 1940.

Stalin was in absolute control in 1929.

He needed cash because he wanted to transform the Soviet Union into an industrial power. To get cash he took the only thing the Soviets could grab. Food.

Stalin stole food from the Ukraine and created a massive famine in the early 1930's. He sold the wheat to the Germans and others. They paid cash.

Stalin used the cash to buy machinery to make steel, power plants, etc. Between 1929 and 1933, twenty five million people staved to death - right on the farms.

The political trials and the army purge followed. In order to get rid of any possible political opponents and military opposition, he murdered many of the top government leaders from 1936 through 1939.

Stalin made a treaty with Hitler in 1939, agreeing not to attack Germany and to provide foodstuffs and industrial products to the Germans. Germany and the Soviets agreed to split Poland. The German invasion of Poland took place on September 1, 1939, the Soviet on September 17. The Soviets denied the treaty existed. On June 22, 1941, Hitler invaded the Soviet Union.

The Germans very nearly won against the Russians. But make no mistake, the Russians, right at the brink of disaster, pushed back and soundly thrashed the Germans.

The War ended in Europe in May, 1945. Stalin was an ally of the United States, Great Britain, and France. All four occupied Germany.

The cold war with the Russians began immediately, as the Russians refused to withdraw from Eastern Europe and took control of their occupied territories as though parts of a new Russian empire.

China fell to the Communists under Mao Ze Dong (modern spelling) in 1949. The Reds were on the rise. The Korean War began on June 25, 1950.

By 1952, the Chinese Communists were eager to get an armistice in place because the cost of the War was enormous. Stalin wouldn't let them and the Chinese Communists had to obey their paymaster. Mao and Stalin did not get along. The armistice was signed after Stalin died. Although the Korean War ended in a political stalemate, it was clear that the Soviets, now a nuclear power, were out to conquer the world, although not just by direct military means.

Stalin had a stroke on March 2, 1953. He died on March 5. He was succeeded by G. Malenkov, a crony Stalin had elevated to power during the Great Patriotic War. Malenkov had splintered support. In September, 1953, Nikita Sergeyevich Khrushchev, the little Ukrainian, took over in a Kremlin coup that ended in the execution of Lavrenti Beria, Stalin's old KGB chief. Malenkov was tossed out of the Communist party, but not shot.

After Stalin, no Communist Party Secretary enjoyed total power. The Politburo and internal, vicious politics limited the role of any one man. Fear of general, political murder and Party purges kept a balance of control in place. The Red Army has not acted in a coup - yet. They might, just as the Imperial Army did in 1917.

Khrushchev did not have Stalin's power. Neither did Brezhnev, Andropov, Chernenko or the present Gorbachev. The Red Army's role is all the more important in light of the possible breakup of the empire. The reason: nuclear weapons.

The old Bolshevik problems of 1905-1917 have returned - they're broke.

Was Lenin murdered? Was Stalin murdered? At first, Stalin was placed in the Red Square mausoleum next to Lenin in an immortal place of honor.

In February, 1956, Khrushchev, then in control as General Secretary of the Communist Party of the Soviet Union, made a devastating, "secret" speech, which leaked right away. He tore away the myth of Stalin and accused him of being a megalomaniac bent on personal aggrandizement and murder.

In October, 1961, Stalin's body was removed from the mausoleum. He was buried in Red Square. Cities, towns, ships, bridges, schools and more were renamed from "Stalin" to something, anything else.

Party Secretaries became the seat of power by Stalin's Example. Lately, Gorbachev has become the President of the Soviet Union. The Communist Party is fading fast and for the first time since 1921, there have been bread shortages in Moscow.

All Party Secretaries have been haunted by the vicious image of Stalin. Lenin talked a lot, but Stalin made it clear - to make Scientific Socialism work, you have to kill anyone who resists, even if it means millions of your own countrymen. Even if it means women and babies.

Millions and millions of them.

Could any man do it again? Khrushchev and the rest could not. Stalin had attacked his enemies in the body politic and the army. The army leadership wouldn't stand for it again.

But, could it happen? Hitler, Stalin and Mao all lived and fought their way to power in about the same era.

It could happen because it did happen, not once upon a time, but once within many of our lifetimes.

Vigilance is the price of liberty.

If you doubt that, take your pointer finger and place the tip against the base of the back of your skull.

Imagine it is the tip of a pistol barrel.

Tap you head one time, lightly.

Vigilance.

CHAPTER FOUR

EXILE, GULAG, EXECUTION

Before reading Stalin's notes, you must understand something about the evolution of punishment in Russia, and the way it was applied to some of the Old Bolsheviks, most importantly, Lenin and Stalin.

The Tsars have been seen in light of grossly inaccurate quasi-history, more as characters of literature than of strict historical study. The Romanov family is best remembered for failure, abdication and finally their own murders after the October, 1917 Revolution.

Tsar Nicholas is often characterized as a weak leader and a personally weak man. He gave writers enough ammunition for those accusations. He botched the Russian participation in World War One to such an extent that millions of Russian casualties can be laid directly at his feet. Not thousands, millions.

The Tsar fiddled while his empire politically burned. He was a reactionary, not a visionary. When the War went very bad for Russia, he panicked. He was immobilized by the thought of losing God-given political power. He lost his life.

But, for all the public concentration on a few isolated incidents of brutality, the Tsars used a gentle whip on their dissident subjects. Don't look at the cascading hemorrhage of death brought on by the Romanovs during World War One. Go back in time.

In 1861 the vast majority of all Russians were peasant farmers called "mujiks." These were dirt poor, almost medieval, serfs. The Tsar freed them that year. This peasant class existed until Stalin almost wiped them out in 1936. Their brutal demise is the prime exhibit of just how Soviet rule transformed Russian life.

After 1861, the anti-monarchists burst out of the social constraints of Russian tradition and theology. The mujiks lived an awful life of toil and hardship. The Tsar didn't kill them - disease did. Disease and unending toil went unchanged by the declaration of their freedom.

But Russia was changing, just as our nation and Western Europe were changing. Cities were developing. Industrial machinery required manual labor. Wages were available in the cities that competed with or surpassed the opportunities on the farms. Moscow and Petrograd became industrial centers. Baku, on the Crimea, became an oil production center. The oil was used to fire industry.

General, public education was unknown in Russia. Illiteracy was rampant. In the cities, however, a middle class began to develop beyond the merchants who traded farm products and the government bureaucrats. This new class was made from the new working class, factory workers and foremen.

This capitalist revolution in new industry went unrecognized by the Romanovs. The Communists saw and exploited it. Factory life was no better or worse in Russia than elsewhere. There was no workman's compensation, no insurance, no medical coverage for workers. Children worked machines. Housing was grossly inadequate. Cholera, that companion of poor sanitation, was a common scourge. But, the same was true in London.

As soon as the mujiks were freed, Revolutionaries arose who called for general murder of the aristocracy by the most violent methods. This was not rhetoric. These people meant murder by any means.

Stalin was born in 1979. In 1881, Tsar Alexander II was murdered by adolescents who threw bombs into his carriage. This was a crack in the mind set of the Russian people - a thunderbolt from heaven! They were mortal! The Romanovs could be killed. They could therefore be replaced - by killing them all!

Tsar Alexander was succeeded by his son, Tsar Alexander III. In the face of political murder, he set up the Okhrana, a secret service intended to identify political problems, isolate the individuals and nullify any threats to royal authority. In the modern age, we immediately think of death squads and shadow murders committed by government assassins.

The Okhrana kept vast files, but they didn't engage in random murder. The Tsar could have had the heads of all the political agitators, but he didn't.

Zealots were sent off to Siberia. Only the most violent or the most incorrigible were executed as a last resort.

The Tsar didn't have political gulags where torture or over-work were the norm. Violent criminals, the ones who actually threw the bombs, were naturally executed. Lenin's older brother Sasha was executed for his participation in a conspiracy to assassinate Tsar Alexander III. Sasha Ulianov would not name his co-conspirators and he wouldn't promise to stop. If he had agreed to calm down, inform on his friends, and stop his campaign of terror, he would have been sent to Siberia. His attitude got him sent to the gallows.

Interestingly, Lenin later remarked that his brother had been all wrong. The point was not to kill an individual Tsar. The goal was to kill off the entire aristocracy, and for that, class warfare was essential, not individual heroics. Many sources indicate Lenin was a physical coward. Sasha was not.

Under the Tsars, mere political theorists were sent packing to internal exile. They were sentenced to a term. If the "criminal" got five years, he would be told to travel to a certain town in Siberia where he had to present himself to the local constable, reporting for exile. There were no chains and bars. The offender could get a job and live as he chose. He had to stay in the area, reporting once in a great while to the authorities, but otherwise, he was free to marry, conduct business or, oddly, think and write about how to overthrow the Tsar.

It sounds quaint.

The Tsar didn't have torture gulags. Once exiled, "prisoners" were over a thousand miles from European Russia, way out in Siberia. There was no telephone, no radio. It was like putting them on the moon. They were out of the way, but they were not idle. Political zealots were known to escape by coming back to civilization where they would be caught by the Okhrana and shipped back to Siberia. They would "escape," return, get caught and be shipped out again. This game went on and on.

Stalin shipped out to Siberia several times before the October Revolution. He would escape, get caught and be shipped back. Lenin did a stretch in Siberia. Many Communists left Russia and settled in peaceful Switzerland. Marx had spent the last years of his life in London, where he remains buried. The Tsar could have reached out and killed them all, but did not. He could have crushed them in 1903 at the London convention where the Lenin-led Bolsheviks took over the Communist party, but he did not.

In January 1905, a peaceful procession of about 250,000 men, women and children tried to present a petition to the Tsar Nicholas II in Petrograd. They wanted food and a little voice in how they lived. Russia had been defeated by the Japanese in a recent war. The Government was broke and had raised taxes to pay for the unsuccessful war.

Father Gregory Gapon organized the march with the authority of the Russian Orthodox Church. The crowd carried religious banners, pictures of the Tsar, but no arms. When they got to the Winter Palace, they found Cossack Guards drawn up in fighting order. The troops fired and used sabers.

Hundreds died in the blood soaked snow.

Revolution began immediately.

The word "soviet" comes from this time. It refers to the council, the immediate level of organization for the Revolutionaries. The Bolsheviks weren't running the show. No one really was. It was born in reaction to the Gapon massacre, known as "Bloody Sunday."

Tsar Nicholas was cunning, however.

If the people wanted bread, he gave them some

bread. If they wanted political power, he gave them a Duma, a kind of parliament. Most importantly, he kept complete control of the army. After "winning" food and a parliament, the Revolution calmed down. The local soviets broke up. People went back to work.

Then, the army grabbed the agitators. The Duma was closed and the bread removed.

So much for the reforms.

If the army had gone over to the Revolution, it would have been different, but the army stood by the Tsar.

In 1917, after a disastrous, cruel war botched by the Tsar, the army went over to the Socialist Revolution.

The Communists did not organize the Russian Revolution. Lenin was in Switzerland, as usual. The Tsar abdicated in the face of the army's defection. The Revolution was produced by wartime misery and international political events. A loose confederation of Socialist groups within Russia organized a government led by a moderate Socialist named Kerensky. The government stayed in the war, fighting the Germans.

The October Revolution is the famous action that established Communist power. In the early morning of October 25 (old calendar), 1917, the Bolsheviks stole the government from the Socialists by an armed coup in Petrograd. Trotsky, Leon Bronstein, the man who had been the wild head of the Petrograd Soviet in 1905, was the brain behind the coup.

He organized the tiny Bolshevik forces to grab key people and locations in the early morning. He took the treasury, the post office, the telephone center and the largest newspapers - all by force. That is how easy the coup went.

Once in power, the Bolsheviks set up the death camps, the gulags, where millions of enemies of the state were sentenced to be worked to death. The Bolsheviks set up the "Cheka," the secret police who were to root out counterrevolutionaries and kill them. The Okhrana gathered information about thousands. The Cheka killed millions. No formalities, no papers. The Cheka just killed and killed without restraint.

Lenin believed in terror. He practiced it. While the killing went on in their midst, the Bolsheviks fought a desperate battle for survival against forces that wanted to restore the former Kerensky government or even the monarchy.

Allied troops landed in the north around Murmansk to try and keep Russia in the War. No prisoners were taken in these conflicts as in many of the political wars of this time. The Reds fought for survival. Ultimately, they prevailed. Trotsky was the victorious Red Army commander.

In 1919, the Bolsheviks went to war with society. They fought all Churches, the middle class, the peasants, the remaining aristocracy, all moderate Socialists, foreigners, and themselves. The Revolution was total war fought by desperate men who had to kill off their opposition to survive.

Somehow, the Bolsheviks did survive. After the civil war abated, they went completely wild. Political murder was normal. Father Gapon's procession, the spark of the Revolution, would have been destroyed if it occurred in 1919. The Tsar's Cossacks had killed several hundred of the protestors. The Reds would have killed them all, not in the street, but in the gulags.

The world and the value of life had changed.

We shudder, today, to think of the killing power of nuclear weapons.

When the Romans defeated Carthage in the Third Punic War (146 BC), they destroyed the city completely, spreading salt on the ground to foul the land for a long time. They killed off Carthage, wholesale. The population was taken into slavery, if not killed outright.

When the Mongols rode from China to Vienna (1260 AD) they left an astounding swath of destruction. Whole populations were wiped out by the Mongol killing machine in order to avoid trouble in the conquered provinces of the expanding empire.

Nuclear weapons are but one way of achieving a historically reoccurring horror.

The Bolshevik killing machine has been unmatched in history by Romans, Mongols or nuclear generals, combined. While Hitler was still in the German Army in World War One, the Bolsheviks were reinventing the meaning of the term "wholesale slaughter." Although he hated them, Hitler openly copied the Bolshevik's terror machine. The SS and Gestapo were modeled on the Cheka which was a combination of secret police and military shock troops. To this day, Soviet Border Guards are part of the KGB, the modern successor to the Cheka. The KGB has tanks and airplanes of its own which are not part of the Soviet military. There is no comparison in the West.

The Bolsheviks offered peace to the Axis powers in the First World War to marshall resources for the Revolution. Once achieved, the Bolsheviks turned on their own people with a vergence unmatched in recorded history. Karl Marx would not have recognized this mutant aberration of his pet theory. But, Marx was dead.

Lenin was alive and well.

Stalin thrived.

The world, always a difficult journey, became a hard place. Perhaps we shall emerge from this nightmarish episode as a better humanity, having seen the depth of potential human depravity.

We don't realize it in the West, but the Eastern Bloc has lived through a calamity equal to the bubonic plague over the past seventy-five years. Death has been commonplace. Life has been depreciated to the futility of meaningless existentialism.

These days, however, the power of freedom is re-emerging. The Soviet Union is on the brink of a deadly civil war, the first to occur in a nuclear power. The Politburo cannot heat or feed the people in the large cities, and they can't rely on the Red Army to cut down masses of the population to enforce the brilliance of Scientific Socialism. Where will it lead?

Wherever brave hearts take it.

CHAPTER FIVE

FAMILY SOURCES

Biographers are often aided by help from the subject's family members. Stories that have not been recorded elsewhere survive within the family unit.

Likes and dislikes, passions and indifference will be uniquely known to family, in ways that may escape friends. Friends may know about mistresses, but family knows the man.

In Stalin's case, the family cannot help.

Stalin was married twice. His first wife, Ekaterina Svanidse died of tuberculosis in 1909. They had a son, Yakov, who was raised by relatives, not Stalin. Some say Stalin loved Ekaterina dearly, and that her death deeply affected him, breaking his heart, making him bitter against life. It could be another propaganda story.

He married Nadezhda Alliluyeva in 1919 and had two children, Vasili and Svetlana.

Alliluyeva killed herself in 1932 at the height of the Ukraine famine. It was rumored she was mortified and ashamed of Stalin's genocide. The press was told she died of appendicitis. Other rumors circulated that she died in a drunken rage of jealousy. At that time, it was unusual for Communists to be buried. Cremation

was the fashion for the godless society. But, Alliluyeva
was buried in the cemetery of a former nunnery in
Moscow. It was consecrated ground! Stalin was affected by her death. He was left alone.

Svetlana has written a book about her father, but
she was never close enough to him in her adulthood to
be a valuable source. Yakov was captured during
World War Two by the Germans. Though offered for
prisoner exchange, Stalin refused. Yakov was killed by
the Germans. Vasili died in 1962, an alcoholic.

There is no "close" family left, because Stalin
wasn't close to anyone, family included.

It is a curosity that no mistresses have surfaced.
There simply aren't any children, grandchildren or
former wives who knew Stalin as adults. Sudden
revelations are made about celebrities regularly - but
not about Stalin. Secret marriages, unknown adoptions,
bastard children: they don't exist. Kerbüssøn is the only
one who ever mentioned the possibility of a bastard,
but wild stories regularly circulate in the gulags. Christ
has been reported as a prisoner. The Tsar is still alive.
The Germans are back at Moscow. It's a cruel reminder
of the hysteria that fills daily, tortured oppression.

No pretenders known to the West have come
forward to date.

He is one of the few characters of modern history
who is so distant from researchers. Even Mao had
surviving family - his wife. Hitler had no children and
killed himself along with his very short-term wife, Eva
Braun, but extensive studies have documented his life
to a remarkable extent. The trail to Stalin, one of the
most powerful figures of all known history, ended
when he died.

Until now.

This is the famous photo of the Politburo after Lenin, in 1929.
From Left to right: Orjonikidze, Voroshilov, Kuibishev, Stalin, Kalinin, Kaganovich, Kirov.

source: US Library of Congress

Yunikidze, Stalin, Gorki   source: US Library of Congress

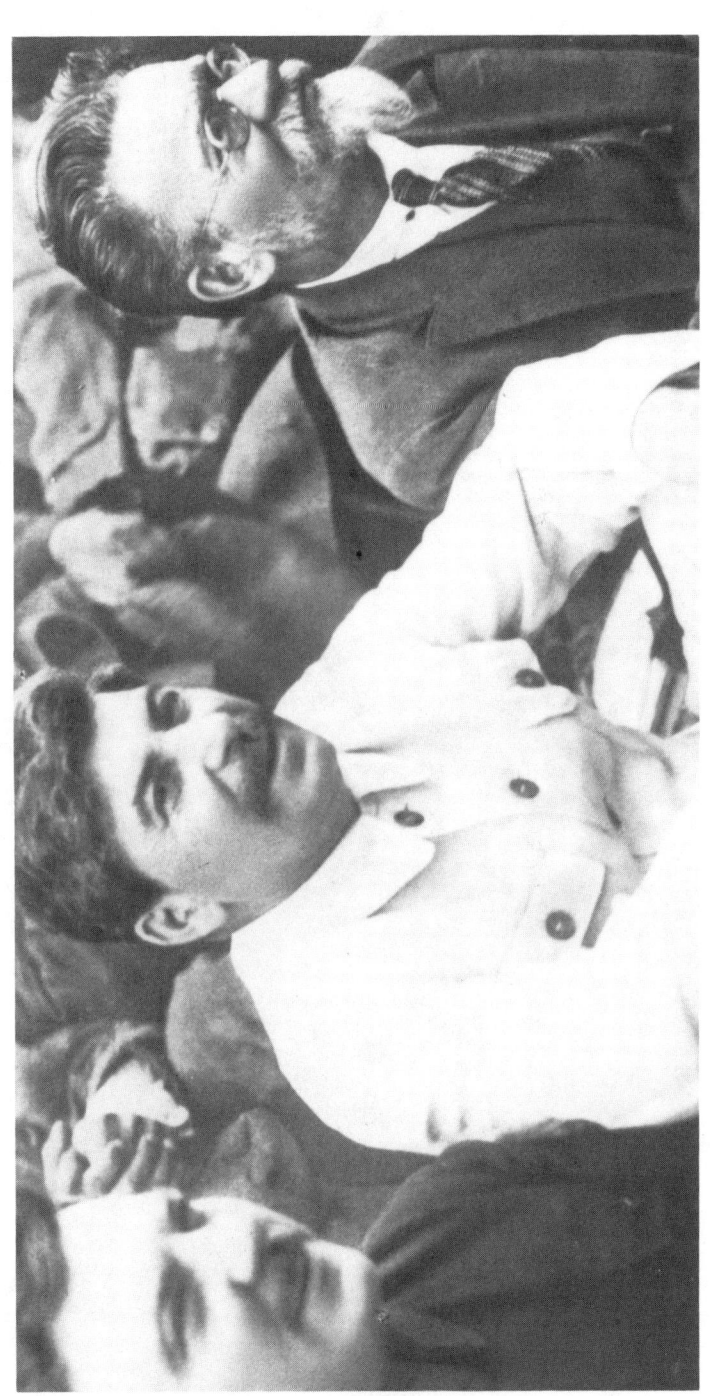

Zhadnov, Stalin, Kalinin   source: US Library of Congress

The Teheran Conference; note Gen. Marshall on the far left. Soviet Gen. Voroshilov and Foreign Minister Molotov are on the far right. Stalin, Roosevelt and Churchill, center.

The Treaty that destroyed Poland, the 1939 Russian-German Treaty. Soviet Foreign Minister Molotov sitting, German Minister Ribbentrop in dark suit beside Stalin.

The 1948 Official Portrait of Joseph Stalin, in military
uniform from the Great Patriotic War.

source: Marx-Lenin Institute, Communist Party of the Soviet Union, Bolsheviks.

"Die Milde Macht ist Gross" from the Haneman Memorial

Genral Jackson Quad in Layfayette Park. White House in the background.

Original Cover of The Communist Manifesto, which was published in London in February, 1948. The text was in German. Subsequent translations were made into various languages.

PART TWO

***

STALIN'S NOTES

Author's note:

During the translations, I noticed a peculiarity in Stalin's use of capitalizations. Country names were properly capitalized, according to correct spelling usage in Russian. We use the same rules in Americanized English. Thus, he would spell "Russia" with a capital "R."

At first, I thought it was a series of mistakes in his scrawled handwriting, but I found a pattern in his spelling. Continent names, such as "europe" began with a small "e."

A misspelling? I thought so, then I noticed he did the same for all continents. He made a reference in one essay to how borders are to be shaped by power, not geography. Land masses may have been fungible to Stalin. Nations were not. I have used his selection of capitalizations.

I have otherwise liberalized the translation, dropping several colloquial, but obscene sexual epithets which translate roughly the same in English and Russian. My substitutions are more traditional insults, such as "pig," or "idiot." Stalin did use those terms in a few passages that remain for the next volume.

On occasion, a passage in the original notes was lined out. It ranged from a few words, to, in one instance, two full paragraphs. I have followed the original intent, and left them out. They will appear in the scholarly edition in the future.

As stated earlier, I have used a special translation method taught to me by a departed friend. In a few instances, for various elements of style, I have relied on M.G. Kerlnakov's excellent <u>Manual of Russian Grammar</u> and Parkham's <u>Slavic Trilogy</u>.

PGF, Jr.

CHAPTER SIX

FAMILY LIFE

I loved my mother beyond words and hated my father beyond imagination. It wasn't that he beat me so often and so hard - I hated him because he couldn't do anything except drink. Then he ran away. He got that right.

I didn't miss him. My mother didn't miss him, but she was embarrassed to be seen as the reason he ran away, for which I hated him all the more. He ran because he felt like it, because it seemed like the thing to do at the time. Once he left, he was free to do as he pleased, which was to drink.

He hated me. I hated him. I can't ever remember liking him. I never did anything to him but be born. That was enough, I suppose. My left arm is useless because of one of his beatings. He hit me so hard with a stick that I got a massive bruise, and then an infection. My arm bones didn't grow correctly after that. I think of him every day because of my arm. My greatest regret is that he died peacefully before I could have him shot.

Once I had my own family, my children, when they could, ran out and left me to my own peace. Both my wives died. My family became the people I knew in the organs of the Revolution and later, the Kremlin. As much as I dominated them, they could not say anything but praise.

I gave Socialist direction and guidance. They gave phoney praise.

I gave vengeance and murder. They gave praise. I gave famine and political upheaval and they still gave me praise.

I brought on the Great Patriotic War, and they gave me praise for that, too.

Wise philosophers make a great mistake. The family is not the central strength of society. Power is.

The family is a weight that drags and eventually pulls you down. It is the hounding echo of conscience and morality.

You are accountable to your family, not your nation. If you care about your family, you cannot be an effective leader because you cannot be as ruthless as the world demands. I've met many leaders in the West who have effectively abandoned their families in favor of meaningless careers, but they are weak men in the first instance because they try to rule through approval, not force. My method is more direct and brutal. Their's is just as cruel, but they haven't the courage to be honest with their wives and children.

Western leaders live publicity lies in pursuit of deceived public approval. I create my own approval.

Subservient workers are a far better family.

They can't get by without you. They depend on you. If you are powerful enough, you own these wretches. You can never own your family.

I've thought about ways to remake the family, but every time I try, something goes wrong. Agitators want the family group structured by biology. I want it set by logical mandate, so that social compatibility and Great Russian reproduction are paramount, with emotion removed. I have tried to meddle in how families are put together, but every program has failed. The same is true of my efforts against the Church.

I have also worked on the idea of a changing family unit. Traditionally, death broke up the family. Then came liberal divorce between spouses under the Revolution. But why should the family be set once and for all by biology and its cousin, adoption? It could be set by lottery every few years so that people could belong to several families during the course of their lives.

This way, even if people cannot find comfort in their lottery family, if they wait, they will soon enough be a part of another family.

Another way is to have the state take care of all children as the only parent, appointing individuals to serve as foster parents for various periods of time.

Still another idea is to achieve the same result by taking up all of a child's time with various government organs. Adolescents have energy and physical size; they make good soldiers, perhaps against you. Draw them away from their families, toward you, by taking up their time. Make their homes miserable, uncomfortable, but offer sport palaces, comfortable theaters, and travel to camps you control. Extend their school hours and seasons. Control the music they hear, the pulp they read and the radio they listen to. Absorb their time with fantasies of their greatness and immortality, and they are yours. Burden their families with work, so they do not have time to undo what you have done. I want children to see me as their father rather than their own biological fathers. If I reach into their homes and drag the children out, I will get resistance. If the children so hate it at home that they run to the state organs for pleasure, I achieve the same result with no resistance from anyone.

The end is the objective. How one gets there is important because one route requires great effort and distraction. Another route may offer slower, but easier results. The target will do all the work for you if you make their entrapment look like a privilege.

Families and government are always at intrinsic odds, except for families in a traditional aristocracy, in which case the families are the government.

Socialist governments require family control to maintain governmental existence and privilege over individuals. Families support the individual, necessarily opposing external control.

There are several ways to forcefully remake the family. The best is famine. If you kill enough of a population, what remains will be fragmentary, without foundation or context. That is the best time to remake the family structure. Hold your model out and offer food to the ones who will cross over to accept your new methods. Let the rest die.

If populations resist, they are your enemy. If you can bend them to your will by force or starvation, then take the next step: make them all your children.

Make all the people look up to you as the all-knowing father.

This is very important.

If you are the leader of a large organization or nation, all your subordinates hate you and look forward to your removal, which allows for their further rise, by one notch. The higher they go, the less room in that one notch for the rising groups. Some must fall by the wayside.

If the broad population are your children, they may hesitate to remove you or support others who would act. If you let up on the pressure and terror, they will rush the barricades and tear you apart. Make the people your children to make them hesitate. In times of action, one man can be killed in an instant's hesitation. In another moment's hesitation, one man can escape. That could be you.

Most people want to be led, but Socialists lead right into disaster. Continued Socialist rule is possible only by terror. It becomes very important to recognize trouble makers and kill them before they can kill you.

In a traditional family, the bond of parent and child, even adult child, will thwart government control. The national leader's power will be limited by this initial, emotional bond. Find it. Kill it.

Criticize it. Attack it. Unleash propaganda against it. Whatever it takes, remove the family unit, destroy family traditions and honor. Make your people your children and they will be less likely to be able to fend and think for themselves.

That leaves your appointed Lieutenants without broad support for their prime ambition - your removal.

Don't let populations pass on religious ideas, property or moral standards. Provide your own substitutes. Use repetition. Keep repeating your rules. Don't let anyone else disclose their ideas. Exclusive repetition, over and over, will eclipse unique brilliance, and convince the masses of anything. Control all means of communication, no matter the shape, size and location of the mechanisms.

Convince children to betray their parents for

actions against your interest. Propagandize children.
They don't know any better. Convince parents to
betray their children. That is a lot easier if the state
can rotate parents and children, removing that emotional bond.

Families will act against you. They will resist.
Villages and towns can have complex, extended family
groups, so that large forces can be brought against you
by prominent families. Destroy them before they
destroy you.

Socialism cannot prosper unless it destroys family
unity in favor of the equal prominence of all members
of society, without preference, which, of course, is
nothing more than propaganda. Socialism forces the
entire population to pull separate oars in the same
slave galley.

Socialist values are incompatible with family
values. I have found Marxist Socialist propaganda the
most useful, flexible and adaptable for maintaining
power. No one can understand it, yet no one in the
empire dares admit their ignorance. In the face of
famine, preaching Socialists look for the greater
common good to come, even if there is none. No,
there is one good to the Socialist in the midst of
famine: his own, well-fed belly.

My biological family provides an excellent example
of Socialist values. I have successfully introduced this
pattern among my Lieutenants. The trouble is forcing
it on the masses. At every turn, with enforced victory
almost in my grasp, I have had to deal with world
events, religion, or attempts on my rule. Therefore,
during the Great Patriotic War I used family unity to
serve the empire.

The traditional family must be repressed and

eradicated.

If the masses don't follow your dictates, have them shot. Have a few shot now and again to remind the masses who possesses and controls real power.

People will notice.

Once you start having people shot, the method must be continued. As soon as you stop, you'll be shot.

The only alternative is to collect your people in high density cities and keep them drunk, drugged or on the brink of economic ruin. Under those conditions, no one will have the energy or intelligence to move against you. This hybrid is starting in the West. I'm going to give it a try in Moscow if all else fails. My only problem is that I have no economic base that the masses are used to. I can't threaten their economic ruin when we are already economically dead.

But, I'll work it out.

I always do.

Koba
1 June 1951

An extant page from the notes, in the original handwriting.
German text.

CHAPTER SEVEN

RELIGION

A committed Socialist cannot accept religion, because no Socialist master on this earth can share intellectual power with God in any degree. All Socialist power must flow from the creations and organs of the state, created by, and answerable to, men.

That means me. Socialists are like bees. They work, work and work. They live and die to make honey which they are not allowed, by their order, to eat. I am the bear. I eat the honey after they have made it. It tastes better that way.

My mother was religious. My wives were also religious. As a boy, I was very religious, which is why I went to the seminary. It wasn't just a way to rise above my class, to escape my geographic cell. I really believed.

I remember studying philosophers in Latin. I read Plato and Aristotle in Greek. Mornings in the Russian Orthodox seminary, I would rise before dawn to walk, pray and think. I have changed. Now I go to sleep at the hour when, as a youth, I would rise. I walk and think, but I also drink too much. My life is thoroughly reversed.

I still believe. That's the oddity. I still believe after

all these years and activity. The resolution: it doesn't
matter. I don't care. I believe, but I cannot live my
belief.

The plague of Socialism is boredom. Once men
are ideologically reduced to accept a common class, the
zeal to excel at work or in thought dies. Through
spies, I have found others in my close circle who
believe. I have had most of those shot, but not just
because they believed.

Because religion and Socialism are incompatible,
I have watched to see which Lieutenant would place
his loyalty more toward God than me. I demand all
loyalty. I enforce that through fear. Men face me and
profess loyalty, all the while hating me. I command the
loyalty of their actions, but can never claim their
hearts. I don't require more.

But once a man shows another that he has a
dedication anywhere but to me, I have to have him
shot. A small crack in a man's loyalty can lead to a
collapse. People can think what they want in their own
minds. I will not allow them to tell anyone else their
thoughts or act on them. I control completely - or I
will perish.

God wants their souls, their thoughts, their hearts.
If God is successful, I must lose. It follows therefore,
that if I am successful, God is held in check in the
battle for that man's mind. If my terror absorbs all
waking thought, I possess the man. I lose him in his
sleep, but he will not move against me in his sleep. I
lose them when they have time to stop and think
about life. The Revolution cannot be allowed to stop,
not because of theoretical goals, but because it will fall
apart as soon as it stops. I have become the Revolution
so that its course depends on my whim. Of course,

that means I have killed the actual Revolution and made it my facade.

I was raised in a Church of tradition and mystery. Evening High Mass in our Greek Orthodox Church in Gori taught me the value of spectacle. We had candle light, incense and chanting. We had murals, gilt and color. We had possessive imagery that would not let go of your thoughts even when you left the Church. Its attraction was a mystical infusion of vitality into one's heart through the comfort of faith and the power of belief. Spiritual life was infinite.

Socialism, on the other hand, extracts power from the individual and dissipates it uselessly amid the volume of worldly confusion. A good Socialist is an experienced apologist. A religious man need never apologize. The trouble is, the religious man submits to God and no one else. He barely tolerates government. As I think back to the grand services in the old Church, I understand that while I did believe, I also had a passion that it all be true - I wanted to believe.

I use that wonderful spectacle now for propaganda purposes. In fact, I have tried to duplicate the Church in our development of Socialism. Well, it isn't Socialism anymore. It isn't anything anymore.

Lenin was an atheist, about the only one I have ever met. But that was because he was too ignorant to think about God. Lenin's denial was purposeful; it was important to him that God not exist. In fact, when Lenin began talking about God, he was intolerable. He wouldn't shut up. Talk, talk, talk. His insistence and unrelenting chatter got to be like a scarecrow shaking in the wind. We all tired of Lenin because he wouldn't stop talking.

But he was wrong. He was wrong so often, we

used to laugh about him behind his back. About religion, he was completely wrong. He could not tolerate the idea that belief was correct. He could not use my method, that is, to acknowledge religion's existence and validity, but then try to capture it. Lenin saw agnostics as a threat, because they might suddenly believe, going out of Bolshevik control. We could tell when Lenin faced a problem he could not overcome. He would keep talking about it, as though it could not exist while his mouth kept going. And going.

Marx had problems with religion. He couldn't explain creation. He couldn't explain the origins of man's intellect. I have used Marx's response in argument countless times, not just about religion, but in arguments about any political issues: "Your question is a product of abstraction."

Just before I executed Tukhachevsky, he asked me why I had to shoot him. He asked why I had taken the Revolution from the Marxist-Leninist course onto my own course of empire. "Your question is a product of abstraction." Following Marx's directions, I removed the abstraction. I used anti-abstractionist methods by shooting him with a real bullet.

Religion proposes hope, offering solutions and comfort. Socialists offer guilt-ridden, endless toil toward some imaginary benefit for mankind which can't be obtained, now or ever.

I offer rewards or torture. Religion is incompatible with my method, so I have regularly crushed it. In taking Church property, I followed the example of the English King Henry the Eighth. In suppressing religious presence, I did nothing different than the Romans did to the early Church. I know the Church will ultimately prevail, because I cannot wipe it out. I can fill it with spies. I can vilify it and make constant propaganda against it, but I cannot defeat it. Lenin could not understand that.

Because I believe, I understand and accept it. The best I can do is recognize the Church as my enemy and maintain constant repression to control it. I have a corral of Moslem, Roman, Orthodox and even Buddhist groups! I am thoroughly outnumbered, but I have the guns.

My old friend Yunikidze once joked that I should create a new branch of the Russian Orthodox Church and install myself as the Prelate. I had Yunikidze shot because he enjoyed private discussions and was prone to saying what was on his mind. I wasn't raised in the Orthodox faith, and my Russian wouldn't sound any better in chant than in speech. Besides, I didn't want to look like I was British. I hate the British. They almost got rid of me in the mid-20's, and Churchill kept trying during the Great Patriotic War.

In the Russian Orthodox seminary, we studied the two great questions men face: where do I come from; where am I going when I die?

Socialism claims the question begs abstraction because Socialism cannot answer it. Worse, Socialism cannot allow thought about the questions without seeing its demise. Socialism is man-made. People are God-made. When I studied the saints I understood that ideas can motivate men beyond logic, fear and greed.

People die for religion. People die from Socialism. If a man cannot be made to fear, he cannot be a Socialist. Ultimately, the meekest Socialist contributes to the creation of an all powerful state, one that holds human life cheap as it regularly declares it to be valuable. Left to its natural evolution, Socialism ends in fascism, the dictatorship of a few over the many in a totalitarian, all powerful government. That's where Bolshevism starts.

When we made the Revolution, we accepted the necessity that many people would die. Many had died in the First World War. But we knew that many more would have to die by circumstance or purpose. When you kill one man, it's murder. If you kill a million, it is a statistic. Hitler killed millions. I killed many, many millions. In the end, I know that my empire will crack after my death, just as the Mongol empire centuries ago. It will crack because my successor will never have the power I have created and controlled. History forbids it.

I don't care.

French philosophers proclaim the importance of today and the speculation of tomorrow. They are right. I live for today. What is past is done. Tomorrow is beyond caring except for crushing traitors against my rule. Nations cannot have a philosophical conscience and hope to survive against men like me. While their leaders debate useless abstractions, I can crush them or wait for them to go broke as they squander their assets on the Socialist utopia that never comes. Socialism is but an academic's antagonistic dream.

Religion is different. Faith endures. Under fire, philosophy turns tail and runs. Philosophers can be killed and buried; then they can be misquoted. Religious martyrs become saints, more powerful in death than life.

Therefore, I believe, but I don't care. My mother believed and cared. She will be in heaven. I will be in hell.

I'll have plenty of company.

Unfortunately, I will have to listen to Lenin again, explaining how religion is a captivating, false abstraction. Perhaps that is what hell will be - endless sessions of listening to Lenin.

As I look back, I rebelled against the seminary because it had regimen and tradition, and I was a young man full of myself. The great attraction of Socialism is that one can be full of one's self, all the while claiming to be heroically suffering for the common cause. I became a Socialist for personal adventure. It was wonderful when it was new. Now, the adventure amounts to nothing. It is tedium. I live to stop others from killing me, which they will ultimately do anyway, just as I did to Lenin.

When I am long gone and forgotten, students will continue to work through seminaries.

But, I know what I'm doing.

If I had stayed in the seminary and taken vows, the Revolution would have come anyway. Another would have stood in my place as the Leader. If it was Trotsky, perhaps all europe might have fallen. I have lived by blaming others for my failures. Trotsky, however, generated regular success. When I got rid of him, I did the world a favor because he would have gone far beyond my borders.

Perhaps that is how I served as God's instrument. Perhaps getting rid of Trotsky was the saving value of my entire life. Maybe I should be called the "Hammer of God."

I shudder that I am beginning to sound like Lenin as I get older and more alone.

I could shake the world and begin again! If I repented and took sacraments, what would happen? But, I can't. I have the old Socialists' disease - I don't care. The young Socialists's disease is omnipotence compounded by clairvoyance, then fortified by immortality.

But the adventure has been glorious!

Eternity listening to Lenin! If I had known that, I would have stayed in the seminary.

Koba
27 July 1952

CHAPTER EIGHT

MOTIVATING BANK ROBBERS

In the days before the Revolution, Bolsheviks were always broke. We tried to raise money from any source imaginable - from donations, selling our incomprehensible magazines, smuggling, pleading, anything. Lenin used to say that while Romanovs had all the money in the world, the people hated them. We had no money, but the people loved us.

He was wrong. Nobody loved us, not then, not now. We were broke because he was always talking about the honor of being broke, how it made us more like the masses than the aristocracy. "A little hunger leads to truth," he would say.

A little hunger leads to more hunger. Beware little, bearded intellectuals who captivate others. They suffer life, from birth. They live to inflict havoc on anyone around them, and they will say the wildest, craziest things just to keep talking, listening to themselves.

Georgians, on the other hand, talk less and act more.

I told the boys I could get plenty of money. They laughed. I reminded them that while they were writing reams of prose, the Bolsheviks were broke and getting worse off. Even intellectuals have to eat. When they asked for my plan, I told them all to wait, to trust me. In the meanwhile Lenin sent some of the boys off to romance the Moscow Schmidt sisters in an attempt to grab their inheritance after the demise of their well-to-do father. What a disaster!

The first Bolshevik converted to capitalism. The second Romeo was successful in getting married. Then the money turned out to be a lot less than Lenin had anticipated. We were a laughing stock. Revolutionary Romeos. I was embarrassed. I took charge of the inbound cash flow.

In the old days, Russia had very little hard money, unlike today where I have presses printing lots of money that has no value. The Tsars minted Roubles that were solid gold. They printed Roubles backed by the same commodity - gold. You could take Roubles and change them into Francs, Dollars or Pounds. When we got Roubles in Russia, we used to smuggle them out to Switzerland so that Lenin could convert the cash to Francs and then spend it all on that rag, Iskra, the Party newspaper.

The BIG money was in the Imperial Capital and regional banks. So I decided to rob the banks. Being an educated lad, I knew I would need help.

Most of the Bolsheviks in 1907 were a bunch a dilettantes. None of them were real fighters who possessed the nerve to carry a gun, enter a bank and rob it. They might talk endlessly about the theory of how to do it, but if they had to actually do it, they would have to bring a spare pair of pants to be ready for the inevitable.

I had to round up a gang of tough activists -

gangsters. Now, dealing with gangsters is tricky. In spite of what they might say, they do it for the money. If you are successful in robbing a bank, will your gang then rob you, take the money and disappear into the background? Fists full of cash are far more attractive than ears full of Socialism. These modern days, when a man has attained riches through loyal Party service we say "Ilyich, for you, Socialism is here!" Socialists love money, too. The problem is that they seldom have it, so they constantly talk about how evil it is.

I went back to Georgia, to the capital, Tiflis, (Russian pronunciation) where there was a large bank. I attended the seminary there. The town has a regular criminal class that will do anything for gold. It did then, and, even though I killed a lot of the locals during the 1920's, it still does. Back then, Georgians relished crime against the Tsar. When I got into town, I knew the problem would be in limiting the number of people who wanted to do the deed. I gathered 15 men in a bar that was regularly filled with mechanics and drivers. I only needed 6, but I couldn't stop them from volunteering. I had studied the bank routine.

Let's return to 1907. Every week, Cossacks guarded a money wagon that made the rounds, stopping at Tiflis as one of many drops. No one had robbed the wagon or the bank in the history of the Empire. It just wasn't done. After all, if you did it, where would you go?

Worse, what could you do with the money since there was nothing to buy? Foreigners couldn't be bothered coming into Georgia, stealing Roubles and returning West to convert the currency for something useful. Too much work. Governments do things like that; ordinary criminals couldn't be bothered. There have been always been plenty of banks to rob in France, England and Italy.

So the Cossacks never expected to be attacked by regular bank robbers. Their polished sabers were for show or for hitting unarmed women and children.

The easiest way to rob a bank is to blow it up. Just blow the whole place to pieces.

The problem is that the money may blow up and burn along with the building. The next best thing is to use smaller bombs to kill the guards, as the radicals did when they killed the Old Tsar in his carriage. If you are going to rob a big bank, you have to kill people. It's just that way.

Regular criminals might stab or shoot someone, but they don't usually blow them up. It's too enterprising! So I had to recruit and then train my little group. I took the 15 men off to the mountains where we worked on making little bombs. I showed them how to carry and ignite them, then throw them. After one week of intense effort, I had my six men.

The others had blown themselves up. The single greatest problem was to stop my 6 candidate robbers from blowing each other up. The best solution was to keep them drunk. I did.

The bank was on the main street. In those days, there were no cars in Tiflis. People moved about on foot or using horses and fat, Georgian mules. The streets were only partially paved with rough stone. When it rained, mud splattered everywhere from trotting horse hooves and the rutting of steel-lined wagon wheels.

The Cossacks kept beautiful, muscular horses that made your mouth water. Tiflis is surrounded by mountains. Peasants raise sheep and an occasional cow, but there was little meat in the regular diet. The best meat in Tiflis trotted in and out of town carrying Cossack asses.

We just waited outside the bank. It sounds very easy, but that is exactly what we did. We had our little bombs, several guns, and daggers, but we couldn't get any horses. As the Cossacks came toward us, they paid nominal attention to several peasants standing idle.

When the Cossacks reigned to a stop, my little band began throwing bombs at them! The Cossacks, like any man, reacted to the explosions with confusion. The bombs worked well. About half of them went off. Three or four were accurate, either knocking the 20 escorts from their horses or sending the horses into a panic, screaming and bucking in the street. There was smoke, shouting, gunfire and confusion!

We took the wagon. And the money. Where did we go?

We stayed in town. I heard that eleven of the guards died. One of my men got it by blowing himself up. The Cossacks went wild when news got out. They came into town and beat people with fury, trying to obtain information. Of course, they also beat people to collect taxes, so their method was not effective because it was so brutally normal. They were not willing or able to commit wholesale slaughter.

We got off with 326,000 Roubles, which, in those days, was a lot of money. No matter what anyone says, the first time the Bolsheviks were taken seriously was when I robbed the Tiflis Bank. Newspapers began to find us interesting, daring. We were a good story. We were brave young radicals who robbed the rich to help the poor. What Englishman wouldn't like that? What Frenchman would not feel attracted to such elan?

After we hid the wagon behind a downtown barn, we got drunk in the bar next door, knocking down a lot of strong, red wine spiced with cinnamon and pepper. I couldn't get Bolsheviks to stand in the street and throw bombs, but I could get them to shoot the bandits after the poor fools were blind drunk. That's how Lenin got food for his intellectual stomach during 1907 and 1908.

No one ever said thanks.

They wanted me to do more. I did.

It was easy until it occurred to the Cossacks that they should try a few tricks to beat us. They used fake wagons. They changed their routes. They cleared streets of ALL people before moving large amounts of cash. Once they began to treat cash shipments as though protecting a member of the Imperial Family, the game was up. By then, we had gotten a lot of cash and even more political notoriety. Foreign governments that wanted to hold the Romanovs in check would now give us a few Francs. When you really need money, no one will give it to you. When you look like a winner, every one wants to help.

I could never get Bolsheviks to rob banks. I had to use criminals and then get rid of them before giving up a share of the proceeds, before they got rid of me! You motivate criminals, just like honest men, by money. With criminals the money has to be bigger and easier - it has to come fast for little work. Danger is not the same as work. Danger is attractive to certain people - usually young ones who don't know any better.

Money, danger, liquor and fame.

You can motivate almost anyone with the right

amounts of those potions. Except Bolsheviks. They live
only for power. A real Bolshevik just won't stop in the
quest for power.

How do you motivate a Bolshevik?

With power over live, defenseless bait.

By 1908, Lenin had spent all the money from the
Tiflis job. Except for my "bankers," we were always
broke, humbly begging support from foreign governments.

I got all the newspaper recognition. Lenin would
then claim the leadership and give endless lectures to
the press. I should have killed him in 1908.

Western europe first heard of my Bolsheviks when
I robbed that bank. We were famous for our daring,
not our politics. Because of Lenin, our politics were
lost amid verbose obscurities.

In Tiflis, most of the Socialists were Mencheviks,
those idiots who wanted a general party organization
subject to the voted direction of the entire membership. We Bolsheviks wanted an elite leadership. Bolsheviks and Mencheviks fought like intellectual tigers
back then.

But everyone looked forward to my bank jobs.
While I took the money, the people got fresh meat.
The horses were butchered as the smoke cleared.

I enjoyed those days. I write these pages today,
reaching back to the past for vitality that eludes me.
Bank robbery was wonderful!

These days I listen to Khrushchev endlessly explain
why Kzakstan can't produce wheat. If you stand still
long enough, wheat will grow right out of your
pockets in that most fertile of places.

I hold Communist Party Congresses where speeches about nothing go on for hours, with many bursts of

planned applause and promises to do more - of nothing. It keeps people happy. No, I mean it keeps Party Members happy.

Socialists. Talk, talk, talk. They can't get anything right. Still I like having Khrushchev around because he is at least uglier than me and he has that amusing Ukrainian accent.

That's what Lenin, the pig, used to say about me behind my back.

It's snowing in Moscow today, white beauty falling quietly, without wind. In Siberia, there is almost always wind during winter. Snow can hit you as if it were little pieces of shrapnel. Fighting nature is futile.

I have learned how to use nature. Only the tough survive. Only the ruthless succeed.

I prefer the clear air of Tiflis over Moscow. I miss the exciting interruption of gun smoke and bomb noise from long ago. It was a grand time of action, beyond politics.

Robbing an entire nation is complicated and ultimately boring if you must live there because the fire of challenge dies out when you succeed. But, robbing a bank -

God, I miss it!

Koba
20 April 1952

CHAPTER NINE

LENIN

Vladimir Ilyitch Ulianov was a pig.

The real work of Bolshevism was handled by several of the boys, and Lenin took all the credit. He had incredible luck. To be short about it, Fanny Kaplan should have finished him off when she shot him. Then, two "strokes" should have finished him off.

But he couldn't make the decision to die, so, ultimately, I finished him off.

He was one of the most boring people I ever met.

I can't recall that he ever, personally killed a man or got into a fight. He always claimed personal heroics were meaningless in the face of class Revolution. Although I never met him, I began to like Sasha Ulianov a lot more than his little brother. Lenin pursued romance but once. Generally, all he did was talk. He became thin as a rail in Switzerland before the Revolution, but then plumped out after his first stroke. Shiftless and permanently aggressive, he could never relax. His eyes constantly darted about when he talked, as though looking beyond the present at events to be. Over the years, his voice got more intense, a little gravelly, and his words became more sarcastic, not just vicious.

Two hour speeches were nothing to him. In 1950, I had the Marx-Engels, Lenin Institute of the Central Committee of the Communist Party of the Soviet Union, Bolsheviks, a Leninist name if there ever was one, publish Lenin's collected works. It added up to 50 volumes after I told them to cut it down from 75! We could have put out hundreds of volumes. All he did was talk and write. And he really wrote his own works! The rest of us wrote a few pieces, but we had ghost writers do the bulk of publications.

When the Revolution was in power in Russia, after we had defeated the Whites and the foreigners, we set out to take Poland. Marshall Tukachevsky was in charge of the military campaign. Although I was originally the Commissar for Nationalities, I was itching to get some military command experience. I was sick and tired of hearing how Trotsky was a great general because of his successes in the Revolution and the consolidation thereafter. But it was because of his military successes that I was very aware that Trotsky was, therefore, the probable successor to Lenin if anything should "happen."

I hated Trotsky and he hated me.

Why? We both knew that the struggle would come down to a match between us. No matter what people say about me, Trotsky would have been worse. He was a born killer, a man without mercy or remorse. His lack of morality and compassion was a defect in his character. I had to learn it over many years.

I needed military success to make my name.

I was supposed to command a part of the Polish Invasion in 1920. Well, alright, I was only the political officer of the flank group of Tukachevsky's forces, but in those days the political officer had authority over military units as well as the nominal military commander. I thought it would be in my interest to take Warsaw before Tukachevsky arrived, so I had my forces move forward at one point and didn't tell Tukachevsky.

Three days later, the Poles counterattacked and destroyed Tukachevsky's army. They went through the gap I had left on his flank. I never got to Warsaw. I barely got out of Poland!

Back in Moscow, the Politburo was very upset. When I returned and naturally blamed Tukachevsky for the misadventure, the boys were almost ready to forgive me in order to save face for the political organs. Then Lenin jumped in and gave me hell. The next thing I knew, I was shipped off to Georgia in 1921 to clear out Menshevik opposition to our Bolshevik government.

I used a page from Trotsky's methods. First, I figured out who the real Mencheviks were. Then I guessed who was probably a Menchevik, but wasn't known to be one for sure. Next, I noted who was only vaguely rumored to be a Menchevik. Finally, I made lists of people who might have had Menchevik sympathies, even if no one had informed on them.

I killed them all.

I shipped their families off to probable death in Siberia in our new gulags. When I left, I had evened a lot of old scores and broken any resistance. I expected to get a medal when I returned to Moscow, and indeed, the boys were happy to let bygones be bygones.

But not Lenin.

He stuck me in the post of Party Secretary, which, in those days, was viewed as a dead end. Me! I had paid for his damn Revolution, and he wanted to humiliate me. But there was nothing that could be done. Dzerzhinsky, the head of the Cheka, the secret police, was still protecting Lenin, who had grown sensitive to assassination after Kaplan shot him.

So, I had to make a plan to get ahead. Actually, I was planning, first, on how to stay alive, when the idea of how to grab power came to me.

The Politburo members loved action and they loved to talk Marxist, theoretical noise, but none of them liked to work. None of them wanted to be responsible for making sure the mail worked, or that there was drinking water in the cities or that the Party system functioned at the lower levels. The boys liked to be off by themselves, like big shots. We had destroyed a government that had grown fat and lazy in the face of easy times. The War destroyed the Romanovs, not the Socialists or Bolsheviks. Once we had defeated the counterrevolution and the foreigners, we had time to relax.

We got fat on our own success. Our terror had succeeded in killing all our opposition. We were masters in the manner of ancient conquerors. Through blood.

I decided to work very hard to make sure the bureaucracy worked. How? By picking my own men to fill slots all through the government. I placed the mail carriers, the firemen, the militia, the engineers, the membership of local soviets and the bulk of the military officer corps below field grade rank. I bought all the grain, created the banking organizations and got the oil for the electric generators. In a short time, I became the source of information from Moscow to the field, and the censor between the field and Moscow. The only one on the Politburo who began to appreciate this was Dzerzhinsky because he had his own organization within the Party, the Cheka, our secret police. Lenin had a stroke in May, 1922. I prayed he would die. The pig lived and almost recovered. But a man who has had one stroke is prone to others, so I knew time was on my side. Lenin slowed down. He gained some weight.

I know what caused his health to finally collapse. It's odd that history has not dug it out. What the world knows about Lenin today is what I have told them for the past thirty years. The man he truly was has faded to the glimmer of dull recollection and extremely particular propaganda, most of it fiction. I have taken special care to shoot all the Old Bolsheviks who might resurrect Lenin's image as a simple man. I made Lenin a modern god, complete with temple!

Lenin didn't deserve it.

Ilyitch, as we called him, was tough. Each day, he ran on and on until he would grudgingly give in to sleep. He ate sparingly and had no time for vices. I don't recall ever seeing him drunk.

His wife, Nadya Krupskaya suffered a glandular condition that caused great discomfort from 1913 on. Krupskaya was no beauty, but she was a loyal servant who cared for Lenin through the lean years.

In 1910, Lenin met a French-born, married woman who had left her Russian husband behind as she evolved toward the free-living, free-loving Socialist model - Inessa Armand.

Armand was born in Paris in June, 1875. Her father died and the family moved to Russia, where many French had lived since the time of Peter the

Great. There was a French sub-culture in Moscow and
Petrograd that had a profound influence on the Romanovs.

Sometime prior to 1905, Armand began reading
Lenin's books and articles. She kept on reading more
of his ponderous polemics. In 1905, after the Bloody
Sunday uprising, she was briefly arrested as an agita-
tor because of her collection of Lenin's publications,
which is how she established her Revolutionary
credentials.

She next left Russia with her husband's brother as
her new lover! The brother died. Amazingly, the
husband supported her with money sent out from
Russia as she enrolled in various universities, trying to
find her position in society. Many Socialists spend their
lives in school as the intellectually acceptable alternative to honest work or dangerous Revolutionary
activity. Lenin met her in Paris in 1910 when she was
at the Sorbonne.

Our dear Ilyitch enjoyed travelling about Europe
in search of collegiate approval. My hard-earned, stolen
money paid for it.

Armand was not a political theorist, nor had she
engaged in Revolutionary acts. When I had the Institute publish the 1950 Lenin Works, I made them use
some of the letters from Lenin to Armand because I
have been toying with the idea of taking Lenin down
a notch in the Party's esteem. It's not that the letters
are passionate. Lenin's passion was politics.

Armand, in Party terms, was no one. Lenin should
have ignored her, but he couldn't.

They were lovers. My people told me so. I could
see it with my own eyes, as could anyone. All of us
were amused by the situation.

Good old Krupskaya didn't mind it. She was like that. Lenin had no passion for her, but he respected and needed her. Ilyitch had an adolescent's infatuation for Armand. He very nearly threw his activism over to marry her and settle into a domestic life! If he had a man's strength, he would have. He probably should have.

He wrote to Armand as he traveled in Europe. He wrote to her from Russia. She was little more than a camp follower, a curvaceous dilettante. But, she possessed what little Ilyitch had for a heart.

After the Revolution, Armand returned to the Soviet Union, amid famine and disease. If one was lucky enough to eat, then typhus or cholera might slash away. In 1920 Armand was living in Nal'chik, which is about 250 kilometers north of Tiflis, up in the Caucasus Mountains. A typhus outbreak took her in September. We brought her body back at Lenin's request and had a public funeral because of her Party "status," eventually burying her in the Kremlin.

I note with some humor that she had tired of Ilyitch, as she did of all her men, and had been linked to efforts to possibly remove him from the government.

Dzerzhinsky constantly set up phoney "resistance" movements which attracted counterrevolutionary fools like flies to garbage. We shot them all. I honestly don't know if Dzerzhinsky had Armand shot without Lenin's knowledge. Lenin could not have ordered it, but he might have reluctantly agreed if pressed by Iron Feliks, as we called Dzerzhinsky. We frequently shot Party members, then said their death was due to disease or heart attack in order to give a public memorial.

At the funeral, Lenin fought to hide his emotions, but I heard him wail in private. He marched with us to bury her in the first cold days of fall. He looked like he would collapse. People noticed his pain. Dzerzhinsky told me Lenin went into a deep depression for several weeks and had to be watched to stop any suicidal actions.

He was never the same. His light step, that pacing while he spoke, was gone. He began to age, and seemed to flicker like a candle burning out. Another man might have suffered a broken heart, but Lenin suffered a broken brain.

I have little doubt that Armand's death led to Lenin's stroke in May, 1922. I had seen him stare into space, daydreaming with more frequency in the time leading up to that May. Obviously, his thoughts were with Armand. Can you imagine his frustration with atheism in the wake of Armand's death? He would stare off as Krupskaya was sitting next to him.

I saw him fade.

As Lenin sank, I saw the question of succession looming. Who would come after the brilliant one? As Party Secretary, I increased the speed of my plan by offering wholesale appointments, not for cash, but for loyalty.

Don't appoint people to posts because they are competent. Find the most incompetent, and appoint that man. When he falls on his face, he needs you to support him. Pretty soon, he'll realize that without you, he's finished. Give great rewards for failure. Make it clear that future rewards depend on unquestioned service. Fear puts him in your corner. His avarice offers you his loyalty, as long as you fill his belly.

I was, therefore, happily appointing the most incompetent people to the most important posts I could control. The boys didn't care. Eventually, all they knew about finance, industry, or the army was what I or my people reported.

The Politburo got fat.

After the first stroke, I started secret talks with Zinoviev and Kamenev, two of the boys on the Politburo. It was easy.

I told them that when Lenin finally died, Trotsky would finish us all off and take over. They snapped it up. The two of them formed an alliance. I sort of jumped on their bandwagon, telling them someone had to run the organizational business while they ran the country.

They started pounding on Trotsky in public speeches and by voting against anything he proposed at Politburo meetings. Lenin started to recover.

One night in November, 1922, Dzerzhinsky met me and we rode in his Rolls Royce through empty Moscow Streets. He liked to drive the big English machine himself. A car full of his Chekist guards tried to stay close behind. The Rolls had an open cab - the driver was exposed to the elements. I was freezing. He enjoyed himself.

Iron Feliks knew Lenin was dying. He was concerned about who would follow. Dzerzhinsky hated Trotsky, but not for political reasons. Feliks had learned through agents that Trotsky hated him. Dzerzhinsky knew that Trotsky would replace him, probably shoot him, if Lenin died.

So Dzerzhinsky made me an offer. He would not interfere. That was it.

He would stand aside and let the struggle commence directly against Lenin. I wondered if Lenin had put the Pole up to this subterfuge, but I knew, just as quickly, that if Lenin wanted to get rid of me, he

didn't need a reason. Dzerzhinsky's Chekists would
come for me, take me to the Lubyanka, and shoot me
in the head. At the time, they had a series of mass
graves about 20 kilometers northwest of Moscow
which they visited each morning with the refuse from
the previous night's interrogations.

As a Pole, Dzerzhinsky knew he could never be
accepted as the Leader. He could be very powerful -
yes. But he could not be the Leader.

I convinced Zinoviev that he should act fast to
replace Lenin and then go after Trotsky. Once he knew
that the Cheka would not take sides, he was off like
a shot!

But he was such a stumblebum that when he tried
to poison Lenin in December, Lenin merely had another "stroke."

Zinoviev, afraid Lenin would find out, hid out by
travelling as much as he could and getting ready to
run away to the West. I tried to get Kamenev to act,
but he was just too dumb to understand what I meant.

I knew that sooner or later, Lenin would figure
things out. If he didn't, Krupskaya would. Lenin knew
the boys were a bunch of clumsy cowards, and he
would see only two people had the nerve and determination to act - Trotsky and myself.

Trotsky would not cross Lenin. He just wouldn't.
But Lenin knew I resented my mistreatment. He also
knew, no matter what the others said, that I preferred
action to cheap talk.

Sure enough, as 1923 began, Lenin started dictat-
ing his political testament, telling the boys that they
should consider getting rid of me! Without saying it
directly, that meant Trotsky would prevail as Lenin's
heir to the Leadership!

Get rid of me! At first the boys couldn't understand why Lenin was concerned about me, because he used to say I was a rude fool from the mountains, practically useful, but politically useless. Now Lenin began to explain that they better get rid of me because I was the one who would act to replace him. He was right. He smelled power.

Timing is everything.

Events happen that can raise or destroy you. You can try to master these events by the most precious plans or you can resolve to be a master of reaction, that is, a man who will review events and make plans as the situation demands and allows. There can be no firm alliances in life because circumstances change. Lenin himself said that morality only depended on what was necessary to achieve success. Nothing that worked to further Bolshevism was immoral. By definition therefore, success couldn't be immoral.

For once, he was right.

I had to act before the next Party Congress, set for April, 1923. If Lenin had his way, I would be the principal subject of the meeting! If he personally condemned me, I would have been shot.

So, it came down to me or him. The boys saw it.

All I had to do was get his cooks, who secretly worked for me, to put more and more salt in his meager food. Salt kills snails and slugs. They explode when covered by salt. So do stroke victims. Lenin, the slug, had another stroke before the meeting. I was surprised - that it didn't happen earlier! This one left him like a vegetable. He didn't speak at the Congress.

I did.

Lenin hung on. He couldn't speak or write, which suited me fine. The more he lingered and suffered, the better. I used to visit him at his little dacha outside Moscow. I had him moved around hoping that would kill him, but it didn't.

Lenin was an icon. I made him that through propaganda. While I was tired of him, I wanted to be sure that his death would be accepted as natural, because he was so much the focal point of the public press. Besides, I didn't want to create the violent precedent of transition through assassination. That would make it more risky for me.

I waited.

Dear Ilyitch kept on living.

One day in January, 1924, Dzerzhinsky and I drove out to see him again. Lenin had a mannerism I detested. When he was about to speak with emotion, he first flared his nostrils and opened his mongolian eyelids a little wider for just an instant. We used to dread it, because it meant he was all fired up and full of himself, ready to endlessly lecture.

He was so incredibly boring!

I was sitting by Lenin's bedside with Dzerzhinsky. We had politely chased Krupskaya and the single nurse away. As long as Dzerzhinsky was there, Krupskaya felt Lenin was safe.

Lenin lay there, physically defeated, but mentally alert, a prisoner within a dying body. He had aged many years. His cheeks were sunken, his eyes, tired. He had lost considerable weight. Bones were outlined against his pale skin. The room was very simple. He rested in a wood frame bed, covered by a gray sheet and a worn Army-style blanket. There was a small, wooden dresser for linen, a large round mirror on one wall, and a square, scratched table with two wood chairs that Krupskaya and the nurse used as they sat with him. The man who claimed to have remade the world to its very foundations looked like a humble mujik, awaiting the embrace of Providence. I was actually trying to be nice. My agents, his cooks, were starting to add salt to his liquid food again, so I knew it would be just a matter of time.

Then the little pig did it.

I was looking at him, telling him how we all hoped he would recover. Lenin flared his nostrils and gave me that momentary glare. I was so angry! The little worm! Lecture me! No more. I jumped up and went to strangle him with my one good hand.

Dzerzhinsky grabbed me, shaking his head. What a sight, me trying to strangle Lenin with one hand! He told me to calm down and pushed me back with his great strength. Without a word, Iron Feliks gently took the pillow from under Ilyitch's head. Then he put it over Ilyitch's face. Dzerzhinsky turned to me and, with a theatrical bow, invited me to proceed. I did. With great joy.

He didn't kick. He didn't twist or push. I pressed down on the pillow, steady on Lenin's face for several minutes. It was delightful.

When I released the pressure, I stood back a step. Dzerzhinsky removed the pillow, then checked Lenin's pulse. He pulled open an eyelid and looked for changes in pupil size as he moved his hand back and forth creating shadow, then light. He turned to me, arms outstretched, and smiled. I smiled.

Lenin's fatal stroke was reported to the masses and the Socialist world wept. We had a grand funeral. I thoroughly hated Lenin.

My success was based on my will to act. Lenin's demise was due to his failure to act. If Lenin had asked Dzerzhinsky to smother me in 1922, I would have died. But Lenin couldn't. Like a fool, Ilyitch gave me Dzerzhinsky's loyalty as soon as Trotsky seemed Lenin's choice for the Leader. With Iron Feliks beside me, I was unstoppable.

Lenin was a pig. So, I had him stuffed.

I made him a god and myself, his political son. The larger his fame, the greater my legacy. It was very effective. The rest of the Politburo couldn't act either. Eventually, I picked them off, one at a time. Me, the little dumb one from the hills.

After Lenin's death, I left Krupskaya alone. She hated me, knew that I was probably involved in Lenin's death, and said some low things about me. But I always liked her. I don't know why. She was harmless and loyal. She wasn't very bright. I guess I felt sorry for her that she had to endure Lenin for all those years; she had suffered enough. More practically, when I let her live, it gave hope to others that they might be able to avoid my wrath if they just tried to please me a little harder.

Sometimes, after the Great Patriotic War, when my Lieutenants and I would drink a little too much, I'd pack them off to see Ilyitch in the early hours of the morning over at "the shrine." I went there for personal inspiration.

I killed him, then stuffed him. My Lieutenants got the message. The masses saw the honor paid to the great Leader. My little circle saw my trophy and took heed.

Appearances can be deceptively satisfying.

I had studied it in the classics. "Divide and conquer." Offer submission, publish praise, then attack with poison. Beware the ides of March.

Several years later, when I had elevated him as high as I could, when I had given him as much power as I could, when I had bestowed as many honors as I could, I had Dzerzhinsky shot. He was reported to have died a natural death. I disarmed him by patronage bribes. But, I had nothing left to offer. I knew he could kill any Leader, because he had helped me kill the Great One. When I knew he must be considering his next move, I moved first.

I liked him.

I didn't have him stuffed.

Which of my successors is like me? Which of my little circle is ready to smother me? Who is the one I would suspect the least, and therefore the one I should suspect the most? Who applauds me the most? Who affects incompetence to beg me for loyal mercy?

Of course, it is my fat little Ukrainian, Khrushchev. But, will he kill me? If he has learned anything, I will die from a "stroke." I have shown favor to Malenkov, giving the impression that he will be my successor. In the next purge, he will fall. The next purge will be the biggest of them all.

In the meantime, one of them may show promise, and kill me.

I hope they don't have me stuffed.

It would be just my luck to be put under a glass lid, next to Lenin. I can't seem to get away from him in this life or the next.

Koba
2 January 1953

CHAPTER TEN

TROTSKY

I learned humility by being beaten up, locked up and treated like a fool. Humility is the time where you plan your revenge, holding yourself back, acting like the subservient dog, all the while waiting for your opportunity to succeed. The truly humble don't act. They have a character flaw.

They ARE dogs.

Political leadership is a special art. The brighter you are, the harder it is to master. Bright people look for sense and order. Hard politicians look for results, no matter the method.

Trotsky was beyond bright. He was a genius. His mind was past my comprehension. Among the Old Bolsheviks at the time of the Revolution, Trotsky was alone, a pinnacle of action and theory. Lenin was smart, but he wasn't nearly as bright as I made him seem after I stuffed him.

Lenin used to talk endlessly. When he finished, his audience would breathe a silent sigh of collective relief. If, however, you asked listeners what he had basically said, they would either shrug or make something up to avoid embarrassment. As Party Secretary, I used to print Lenin's statements and the official "interpretations." I just made them up. Lenin was a windbag.

Trotsky was not.

Lenin was a weak individual. The Germans knew that and helped him move through Germany from Switzerland on the famous sealed train in 1917 for the trip to Russia. They counted on him to be one of many forces weakening the Russian will to fight. The Germans didn't know much about Trotsky. If they had, they probably would have shot him because he was so dangerous. He was a genuine Revolutionary.

In 1905, Trotsky led the Petrograd Soviet in the first step of the Revolution after the Gapon massacre. Trotsky organized and ran their Soviet for its brief existence. He did something unique - he pressured the Romanovs. He showed their frailty because he revolted and lived, even if in exile outside the country for a while. When the 1917 Revolution began, it was a child of the 1905 action, intensified by the failures in the First World War which caused the army to go against the Tsar.

When the Tsar fell, Trotsky was in America, living in the Bronx, New York City under his real name, Leon Bronstein. In May, 1917 he returned to Russia.

Lenin was floundering. He had been in Petrograd since April, sometimes hiding from the ever present rumors that the Kerensky government was after his head. Lenin had German money behind him. He was supposed to be knocking down the Kerensky Socialist Government, getting them to pull out of the War.

Lenin didn't know what to do. In fact, Kerensky pushed Lenin around and threatened to arrest the Bolsheviks.

When Trotsky came, things changed.

Trotsky took charge of the muscle, the small group of troops that the Bolsheviks had. He stopped the Socialist harassment with occasional street fights. He organized and recruited. Sometimes, at political rallies, he would speak first. Then, we would start signing up new Bolsheviks while Lenin was speaking. The longer Lenin spoke the more men we would sign up, probably because they felt like standing and stretching their legs, anything but listening.

In May, 1917, we had a few hundred. By early October, we had thousands. We had arms, a headquarters, and a plan. On October 25, Lenin finally agreed to use troops to crush the Kerensky government. Trotsky had been after Lenin to act for two weeks. The only reason Lenin finally agreed was Trotsky's insistence that the Socialists were going to arrest and shoot Lenin before he had a chance to run away again. Lenin was terrified.

He let Trotsky go.

Trotsky delivered Petrograd, and eventually all of Russia.

I used to watch these two men with awe. Lenin, because he was so indecisive, Trotsky because he was so vital, yet acting under Lenin's "direction." After a while, I found a fatal character flaw. Trotsky, while unsurpassed in ability, lacked focus. He didn't know what he wanted.

He achieved, but had no concept of how effective action should deliver personal power. As the Leader, he would have to concentrate on the result. He would not be the general, the performer. It dawned on me that his leadership of the Petrograd Soviet in 1905 had never been intended to lead to personal success - he wanted to form a larger entity, a government.

He was Menchevik, through and through, no
matter what he said about agreeing with Lenin's choice
of an elite cadre. Trotsky was willing to be ruthless to
attain victory, then hand over the power to a government outside his control. He could lead troops, but he
could not lead a government. He could be an advisor,
but never the final executive.

In the end, he was afraid of being alone at the
top, and felt effective politics beneath his manifest
role.

Pride was his critical flaw. He wanted to be
Cincinnatus, fulfilling his duty when required, otherwise subservient - but constantly praised.

In 1917, I began to praise Trotsky whenever he
was present to see his reaction. He would light up. He
would stand taller, his eyes brighter. If I criticized him
directly, he would smoulder with anger. If I complimented him, but did not praise him, he would look
hurt, disappointed. I found his weakness while he was
in the full sweep of his glory - pride.

Trotsky would not have harmed Lenin or removed
him. I think Lenin sensed this as well. After the
October Revolution, Trotsky created the Red Army
from very little. He won one of the greatest, most
savage conflicts in the sweeping history of military
conflict. He stood by Lenin in the face of the 1921
famine. Trotsky had the army and could have blown
the Cheka aside like a puppet. He had the power.

But his pride would not let him reach out and
take the leadership. He wanted it to be pressed upon
him by the others as evidence of their acclaim. He
wanted the Politburo to demand he accept the post in
recognition of his achievements.

He didn't realize that was impossible. Political

animals like myself grab and possess power. Brilliant fools like Trotsky think they will rightfully have power after they earn it.

It will never happen.

While I was gathering strength in the political bureaucracy, Trotsky was basking in his war success, doing nothing. I was demanding pledges of loyalty from the bureaucracy; he gave away his loyalty to a dying man.

When I smothered Lenin, I also killed Trotsky's pride. Once Lenin was dead, removing Trotsky and then killing him was easy.

I had gathered my strength all through the Party before I got rid of Lenin. When I moved, I had the support of the functioning government. If Trotsky had used the army, he could have blown me aside, but I thought he wouldn't. He couldn't. He didn't want the leadership. There was no one to use the army for because he wouldn't use it for himself.

Once he hesitated, I moved against him, quietly, slowly at first, then more openly. The trick was to convince the Politburo that Trotsky was going to get them all, kill them and seize power. All I did was paint a picture that was already in their individual minds. I would tell each of the boys, in hushed confidence, "He has the army, he has power, he is going to get YOU."

The Politburo reacted by moving against Trotsky, His supporters were sent on useless missions, now that the battles were over. Many never returned from those phoney trips. We used to give them railroad tickets and a big sendoff at the train station. At the first stop, the Cheka would drag the Trotskyite from the train and shoot him.

Meanwhile, the government began bribing military

leaders with promises of wealth, promotion, special postings or lies of Trotsky plots to seduce their faith in Trotsky away.

We started rumors about Trotsky stealing army money and supplies. Other rumors spread that he was a homosexual, a German agent or a secret monarchist. We pounded away with rumors and false accusations.

Repeat them long enough, far and wide enough, and they become truth. I controlled the press, the radio and the movies. All the Politburo had to do was neutralize the army. The Politburo didn't need the support of the army - they needed it to be neutral. Dzerzhinsky had already told me he would oppose Trotsky.

Trotsky saw the plan unfold, but couldn't believe his comrades would act so shamefully. We did, gleefully. He did nothing.

When it became clear that Trotsky was nullified as a power, I finally moved against the rest of the Politburo.

I used the same tactics we had used on Trotsky. My bureaucrats sent Politburo flunkies on useless, one-way journeys. I cut off funds for departments outside my control. I literally cut off the lights, too, in their offices and homes. Soon enough, Zinoviev, the coward, changed sides and began teaming up with Trotsky.

They wanted to get rid of me. It was too late. While I kept the Politburo busy fighting with Trotsky's imaginary ambition, I worked on finishing the Politburo.

In 1928, I had Zinoviev and Kamenev booted right out of the Communist Party. Best of all, I had Trotsky arrested and exiled under close arrest in Alma-Ata. I finally had Trotsky kicked out of the country in 1929.

I hated Trotsky. I thanked God, however, that he was so powerful, yet so limited in practical ambition. A less intelligent, but more ambitious man would have destroyed me.

Ambition, not intelligence, rules. Persistence, not pride, prevails. The world is cruel, but such is its method for survival.

Trotsky made the Revolution work, then he delivered it into my hands because he didn't know what to do with it. I would have had the Cheka shoot him in 1929, but I did not want to abuse his influence overseas. I wanted to appear magnanimous in victory. I also did not want to create a martyr, yet. His voice would have been too powerful. He lived.

As with Lenin, I did not want to develop precedent for outright murder of Party members within the Politburo, especially as I was the next Leader.

Trotsky lived in poverty, writing useless polemical books that did not affect me in the least. He roamed from country to country, eventually moving to Mexico. My Chekists were driving him crazy by killing off his old friends and family, quietly, and most importantly, one at a time.

I didn't care to physically torture Trotsky. I did want to make him an example, however. I had to make the point that I would extract vengeance anywhere in the world, over great time, with summary cruelty to my enemies and their families.

It worked.

I decided to finish him off because he was writing a book - about me. My Chekists murdered Trotsky in 1940 in Mexico. An agent smashed his skull with a hammer. The book was published in 1941, and is called "Stalin." In his poverty, he was desperate to make money by any means. So he wrote. He was a compulsive, a person driven by uncontrollable forces. Trotsky couldn't stop complaining. His whining was unbecoming.

Most of the book is inaccurate drivel about how life was unfair to Trotsky and how I wasn't as good a performer as Trotsky in the Revolution. I wasn't. So what?

The point is not to be the most visible or most vocal, as were Lenin and Trotsky - the point is to be the most effective. Don't worry about making a lot of speeches or leading armies. People forget words and achievements.

They don't forget who feeds them. They don't forget that if you gave them the roof over their heads, you might take it back. They don't forget you if you have shot their neighbor, commanding officer or comrade. History can be written as one pleases, and then rewritten as one later requires. Inconsistencies are forgotten. There is no objective "history."

Power is now and tomorrow.

Yesterday is the apologist fop's domain. Anyone can lay claim to it. I don't care about it. While it is true that history repeats itself, people don't have the time to read history, think about it, and then find the courage to apply it. I did. I made the time. When the others were out making noise and posing for pictures, I stayed behind to think and plan, then organize.

Political martyrs are made by assassination at a sensitive time. If the assassination is postponed, the martyrdom fades. It may never attach. Trotsky was so pre-occupied by my pursuit that he could not organize against me inside the country. He had to move from place to place, country to country, remaining on the defensive. When he died, the outcry was short and meaningless. No one in Russia said a word. More importantly, no one in Russia stirred. I didn't care beyond that if the rest of the world stopped for a period of mourning. I crushed one of the most powerful men in history by a slow, but relentless pursuit. I took history from his destiny by making him seem smaller and smaller as time went by.

A brilliant man can do dumb things. I'm laughing as I write this. Let me explain.

In 1934, Trotsky was making his usual, meaningless noises. He got in touch with the Japanese and Germans to see if they would back him in an effort to retake the Soviet Union - from me. In exchange for their aid, he promised to give them territory, very much in the way Lenin had promised the Germans that he would take Russia out of the War if they helped him attain power in 1917.

The Germans thought Trotsky was crazy, and they promptly leaked the discussions to us. The talks went on. The Germans asked Trotsky to tell them who would back him within the present Russian Government if he started a counterrevolution. He gave them a list of 35 names!

I had the list inside of 24 hours. When arrested, the 35 had given the names of over 200 more. I shot them all. I shot their friends and family. I shipped more off to the gulag.

With opposition like Trotsky, I didn't need the NKVD to root out the problem, just to get rid of the bodies.

Trotsky couldn't shut up.

I have observed great leaders throughout this century. I have been a foe to all, friend to none.

Without any doubt, Trotsky was the most brilliant and productive of them all, but he was the most politically impotent. He had the world in his grasp and could not seize it. When I had him killed, no one cared.

Ultimately, when I had no further use for him, when I didn't care to play with him any longer, I took my revenge.

I won.

Consider that last point. The desired result of any political action is to win. The most profound political action may be the result of a personal desire, unknown to history.

Koba
27 September 1952

CHAPTER ELEVEN

HITLER AND
THE WAR

We call the Second World War "The Great Patriotic War." I invented that invigorating name as part of a propaganda campaign.

I blame the War on the American President, Woodrow Wilson; certainly not myself. I didn't want to have the War. It almost cost me the empire.

After the First World War, the Germans were soundly defeated. The Revolution had taken hold here. We were defeating the Whites and dealing with the foreigners. By 1920, we were back into Poland. The Great Powers should have dealt with Germany more intelligently, but they were fools.

All europe was hurt by the War. If not touched by shells, economics came to bear. The War had to be paid for. Europe went broke. The governments that had been so haughty were now humbled.

The most wealthy nation in the world became the United States because she was the merchant of munitions for the Allies and was untouched by the fighting. The British and French owed her billions of Pounds, Francs and Dollars. If the British had been in that position, they would have made europe their colony. If the French had been the great creditor and emerging power, we would have all had to cower, and learn to speak correct French as they occupied us all. But the United States was different.

Wilson couldn't make decisions. He was a professor, not a leader.

First, he couldn't figure out that the War was a great conflict and that the resolution would offer an opportunity to undo the Bismarck creation of modern Germany. Then he couldn't understand how to fight the War once America came into the conflict. He placed American troops under Allied Command where they were used as fodder. The English and French used their own troops as fodder, too.

The great Allied generals didn't get results after all the troops were consumed. They kept on needing and getting fresh troops.

By causing the Revolution here, in Russia, we did more to hurt the German War effort in the First Great War than the Allies did in the field. We caused disenchantment behind their lines in greater magnitude than the War's primitive attempts at civilian bombardment. We built the Red menace in Germany because we were determined to export Revolution there, tearing down another, related monarchy.

In war, troops eat first. Civilians eat if there is anything left over. When the German civilians got hungry, they began to see us, the Reds, in a different light. They began to look at the motives for their War. Their resolve weakened.

A hungry stomach supports Revolution unless the established government is willing to kill the potential opposition, thus getting rid of the hungry stomachs.

But that was the difference. The Germans could not bring themselves, at that time, to kill their own people in sufficient numbers to destroy civilian unrest at home.

The Kaiser, cousin of the Romanovs, resigned and went to live in Holland at the conclusion of the struggle. The Germans felt betrayed. They were! The War had nothing to do with their interests. War does not serve the interest of the broad population - only part of the population, not the army, stands to gain.

The Allies obtained victory in the field because the German bureaucracy gave up. The Wermacht was not defeated in a climactic battle.

The Allies should have crushed them. Once the German Army left the field, the Allies should have continued the War against the German nation, destroying it. Large parts of the population should have been dispersed. I would have been happy to offer Socialist instruction in Siberia for millions, for a fee from the Allies. German land should have been seized and given to French and English peasants for new settlement. French and English factories should have been able to draft German labor for any wage the factory felt like paying.

If they did not destroy Germany and the German people, then the Allies should have been generous and done them no harm at all, as though the War had not happened.

The French and English did want to destroy Germany, but the methods they proposed were not enough. Wilson made the Allies water down the post-war poison. It wasn't the borders that mattered. The Allies, like typical capitalists, wanted money. They demanded reparations. Ransom. Ransom does not work.

All through the middle ages, european wars were fought for ransom. Once paid, ransom calls for revenge. Ransom is useless. Whatever is paid must be spent in building arms to fight off the probable revenge.

Wars are fought to be won. When you win, kill off as many as possible. Then take whatever you want. Don't let the war end. Keep up the killing. Keep taking. Keep the loser on the defensive forever. As soon as you stop, revenge will be born. It will grow and grow. Like a fire, it will absorb all around it.

The Germans, beaten in the field, were not beaten at home. I tried to pick up where the Allies left off, but I couldn't win. The Germans were starving after the War while they paid reparations, but they were not dying out. The starvation was only temporary, not genocidal. I would have starved millions. The Allies only starved thousands, just enough to whet the survivors' appetite for revenge.

Worst of all, the Allies did not shoot the leadership of Germany. Professors, Wermacht officers, newspapers owners and editors, politicians and clergy should have been shot. I would have done it. The Allies could not. The British might have, but Wilson wouldn't let them.

Too bad.

We spent a lot of money trying to get the Reds to grab control in Germany. We used guerilla forces. Unfortunately, so did the Germans. We used murder. So did they. Eventually, the Nazis came to power as German Socialists opposed to foreign Communism. We learned a big lesson from that.

Our Reds were just that - ours! They were under control of Moscow. It was 100% control, the way

Lenin had taught.

We should have done it the other way, the way I do it now. We should have declared it a local war of national liberation and developed a Communist movement in Germany that had many topical differences from the Soviet model. We should have taken out the international element and used only Germans in the organizational apparatus. They could have foreign advisors, but not foreign members in their local Party.

We made a mistake. It wasn't just my mistake. Lenin and that genius Trotsky had their own formulae about the power of ideas. They were the ones who insisted that Bolshevism be spread by international forces.

People don't really care about international forces. Professors do. Intellectuals do. But professors and intellectuals are a dime a dozen. In a fight, they will turn and run. They are not crisis leaders.

Without leaders, troops will not fight. Without leaders, troops have no discipline. I had a gut feeling that the German movement should have been run by prominent Germans at all levels, under our control of course, but otherwise, for all the world to see, a "German" movement.

The Germans wanted to replace the monarchy with something different. The battle came down to elements of various Socialist groups fighting with my Reds and among themselves.

Socialism promotes a powerful state, one capable of serving the theoretical welfare of the people with all manner of service and protection under the rhetorical umbrella of "the common good." To finance that, the state must have an interest in all economic activity either by direction of the resources required for production, or taxation. The larger the state, the more control it must have. Soon enough, people realize the state acts for itself, its own interests, its own welfare, before theirs. By then, it is too late.

Socialism is the slow tide that drags even the largest ship into fascism. As Bolsheviks, we by-passed the evolution of fascism by declaring the right of a strong elite to control the destiny of the masses. I cut down that group of "elite" leaders to one - me. With Socialism, government evolves more slowly, day by day, becoming larger and larger, more and more strong and self-serving. It becomes a monster, then turns on its supporters.

Several of the German Socialist groups would have ended up as fascist dictatorships had they succeeded in getting power. The fact that Hitler won out was testament to violence. We Bolsheviks began mass killing in 1917, right at the start of our governmental power. Hitler couldn't begin until he had gotten control of the state. It took him years.

We took control in a coup. The German people gave Hitler control. I tried and tried to win the intellectual battle with the German Socialists, if not the localized gang battles.

We lost on all counts.

Lenin, as usual, was wrong. Germans will not accept a Russian master without a fight. They gave us one. We lost the international street battle in the early 1920's, but I used the lesson later, in China. Germans are not internationalists. They regarded us as foreigners bent on conquest - exactly what I am.

The Nazis and Hitler were Cossacks, but as German Cossacks, they were accepted by the rest of the Germans. Russian revolutionaries could not be accepted. There are no european comrades. That was Lenin's dream. He made it up. Marx made it up. A French Communist has little to do with a Russian Communist if fighting breaks out.

Hitler became very much like us. I don't know if he was truly that way to start, but he was certainly a student of our methods. We had succeeded in the face of worldwide opposition, famine and counterrevolution. He saw that. He also saw how we consolidated power by systematic terror. When the Bolsheviks were losing in Germany, the Nazis were one of several German Socialist groups that had beaten us. Their ultimate emergence was not assured until they began to use our methods on their own people. I knew I could deal with Hitler once he began to act like me.

Running Russia is a hard job. It takes time to get control and constant effort to keep it. The Revolution can't end. If it stops, the people will toss me out because they will have time to see how bad off they are.

Conquest is more a matter of opportunity than just military force. There is no political seed in the hearts of men that calls for the establishment of loving, socialist regimes. There is no such thing. Conquest under the old Mongol system was a matter of killing everyone, by use of only military force. If the population was dead, there was no chance of revolt. On the other hand, what good is conquest unless you have a population ready for exploitation? Who will do the work? The Mongols didn't have possessions except for their horses and a tent. I have sixteen houses, wealth beyond imagination and power that is permanent; well, as permanent as I am. While I can kill a lot of people, it doesn't make any sense to kill them all. Therefore,

means other than military force must be productively
employed.

Once Hitler won, the Germans were in for it. I
knew it, because once the Revolution came to power
here, the Russians were in for it. Political doctrine
wasn't the issue. Bolshevism was a radical political
force run by a small group, and only a small group.
Terror was acceptable to achieve and hold power. The
same was true of the Nazis.

I knew Nazism couldn't be exported politically
because it was inherently German. The Germans had
been defeated in the First World War and I figured it
would take Hitler until 1945 to gather enough economic power to even think of going to war again.
Then he would turn against the ones who had embarrassed Germany - the British and the French. They
would exhaust each other in another war.

Unlike the Tsar, I had no desire to be sucked into
the conflict by some useless alliance. When it was
over, I would have the largest army in europe. I would
have money from selling munitions to one side or the
other.

And I would have europe.

I didn't want to go to war. They would hand it to
me.

I didn't care what Hitler did, as long as he did it
first to the Germans, then to the French and British.

I was happy to have the German Wermacht and
Luftwaffe keep secret bases in Russia during the
Weimar days because we got paid for it, and it was
harmless. It also helped to train some of my military
people.

Yes, I knew that Hitler wanted to have a chunk of
the territory in the Soviet Union for his so-called

"lebensraum," but I thought he would go first against the other europeans before attempting to go against us.

From 1936 through 1939 I killed off a lot of the leadership of the armed forces. They weren't doing anything, anyway. An army in peacetime is a dangerous thing. They sit and talk: about the problems with the political leadership!

Armies live by tradition. The only tradition we had was the Tsars, which was not helpful to me. So I didn't wait to hear of plots. I just assumed they were there. My Chekists took care of the details. It worked because for every general I shot, there was an anxious colonel waiting for a promotion. Trotsky explained to me that sergeants really run the army, not the generals. I could shoot all the generals I wanted. I took good care of the sergeants. No military plots against me ever existed. I got them first.

I didn't mind disrupting the army because I had no effective enemies. I made a secret deal with the Germans in 1939 to take Poland.

I suppose nothing is secret in government, but this was a private agreement that I denied then and I still deny to this day. I keep telling people it never happened. If someone insists it did, I say it is an invention of the Roosevelt-Truman CIA bureaucracy. True intellectuals will always accept my word over their own government's announcements because I pander to their pride as fellow soldiers in the cause of "truth," and because they have an odd disposition, like an adolescent child, to disbelieve their own government in favor of any other source.

I sold a lot of wheat to the Germans. I also sold oil, steel, leather and more. They made the deal with me to keep a friend at their back. I knew they would push off, west. I was delighted to get half of Poland back into the empire. I hated the Poles because they defeated us at the time of the Revolution and defeated me in the Tukachevsky offensive. This time, I took the country the correct way. I had the Germans do it. I made a great deal. For agreeing to stay out of the fight, I got the Polish Ukraine. We signed the treaty on August 23, 1939. On September 1, The Germans invaded Poland. We did it on September 17.

The Germans destroyed the military power of Poland in two days. England and France declared war on Germany on September 3. They left me alone, even though I got half of Poland from Hitler.

It was wonderful! They were going to fight among themselves, not with me. Hitler was not functionally prepared for war. His control of Germany was not near my control of Russia.

He made up for it very quickly. I couldn't believe it. He rolled up France in no time and chased the British right back to their island. His commanders used mobile armored units as shock troops to smash through the best defenses in the world. We were all very impressed.

I let my army invade Finland in November, 1939. They wanted to show off. Four months later, after massive casualties, we prevailed, but I had to shoot a lot of generals because they performed so poorly. It was supposed to take 12 days. I was not looking for a fight - just a quick victory. Instead, it was very embarrassing. All I wanted was a wedge of territory and a few navy bases to protect Leningrad. I got them.

If I took the whole country, I might have been denied credit in the London and New York markets. In order to show how generous I was, I left Finland alone in 1940 and even in 1945, after they had sided with the Germans.

Anyone who occupies Finland is asking for trouble. It costs too much. The real prize in the modern world is oil, not reindeer. Besides, we have all the cold air we need. These days, I would love to have a dacha in a place like Cuba. Warm breezes, good food and great cigars. Back to Hitler.

I was embarrassed by the Red Army in Finland. At the time, Hitler had started killing Germans with his Gestapo and SS. I was flattered that the Gestapo was openly modeled on our Cheka. We had changed the name of our security organization so that it was now the NKVD, but it was still the same Cheka. Hitler was purging his Wermacht in the middle of the war! That is not the best time to do it. Wait until it is over. Then fire the most successful officers in case they decide to look for campaigns against you.

Some of my people began to tell me they thought Hitler might go against us sooner than we had planned. I rejected that, only because I had such fools working for me, I routinely rejected all their suggestions. The intelligence data became harder and harder.

Our spies were everywhere. But target governments know they cannot stop spying altogether, so they use spies to send back false information to the spymaster, hoping to turn the game around. Therefore, any information obtained by spies is suspect. Further, one's own Lieutenants may use a "spy," as the "reliable source" for information they have just cooked up to further one of their pet causes. When I began to hear from our spies that the Germans were thinking of coming east, I naturally rejected it.

How could they come east when they were still
fighting in the west?. Further, Hitler would need a few
years to start killing off whole populations and breaking down the national character of the occupied
countries. How could he suddenly start east?

Was he crazy enough to leave the English intact,
at his back?

As I found out, Hitler was crazy.

On June 22, at 3:15 AM, German soldiers crossed
the border. They faced little opposition as my forces
were only just getting alert orders.

I was wrong.

On the first day of the War, we lost over 1,200
aircraft. I had more troops than the Germans, but I
had flunkies as commanders. So I had a small stroke
from June 23 until July 3; so what? The circle of my
Lieutenants was so weak, they didn't have the courage
to shoot me! It goes to show that as the Leader,
always pick weak followers. You'll live longer.

When I calmed down, I knew what had to be
done.

Hitler was a Mongol in modern clothes. He killed
off masses of people everywhere his forces went.
Would we lose the Ukraine? Maybe, but once the
Germans got in they would be busy killing off the
Ukrainians instead of getting them to help. The
Germans would be busy killing everyone around them.
That was fine with me, because it would slow them
down. It did.

We finally turned to fight at Stalingrad in August
1942, then at Kursk. The Wermacht knew they were
finished when they saw me use Asian troops, Moslems,
Kurds, and other nationalities. The Germans were
being killed at a great pace. They did not have replace-

ments. I had replacements from the depths of Soviet Asia, not just Russia. In December, 1942, the Germans got within thirty kilometers of Moscow, to the suburbs. I appointed Zhukov as the military commander and gave him free reign with all our men and supplies.

Zhukov gave me Germany. He never made a move against me. Even if we had lost Moscow, we would not have lost at Stalingrad or at Kursk. We would have beaten them anyway. I stayed in Moscow during the battle because it occurred to me that my flight out might break the delicate balance of terror. The military might try to replace me if I ran out on them again. I did have several planes ready, just in case.

Unfortunately, I now had to have generals. That was dangerous. So, I became the head general. As long as I had Zhukov, I didn't need any other top commanders. I was the Generalissimo; Zhukov was my personal general. The rest were his generals. He kept them straight.

The western area of the empire was destroyed by the Germans. As I saw things, the disaster would lead to new opportunities. There were new areas to he had. Bulgaria and Hungary would be occupied. The coast of the Adriatic would fall. Would I have Turkey, Greece or Italy? I hoped so.

After Moscow and Stalingrad, I had the ability to continue the fight. The Germans did not. Zhukov was going to grind them up, no matter the cost to us. I knew the rewards would be worth it.

In 1939, when I let the army go into Finland, I had to be careful not to offend the great Western powers. By 1942, the Allies needed to keep me happy. Russia had made a separate peace in the First World War. I let out rumors that I might consider the same action. England and the United States now had to take steps to help me out. It was the first time we were able to get into the Western credit markets and sell debt as a respected government upholding the world order - of democracy!

Having been double-crossed by Hitler in 1941, I was careful in my dealing with the Allies. I knew Churchill would stab me in the back if he had the chance. He hated Bolsheviks beyond reason. But Roosevelt was the Allied boss. He had all the money.

It has always been hard to gauge American leaders because they change so frequently. They live in a public display making it hard to understand what they really mean amid all the talk. Often, they talk and don't mean to say anything.

After Stalingrad, I was trying to devise a way to get the Allies to agree to let me take large parts of eastern europe. I was prone to avoiding armed conflict, if possible, but I didn't rule it out altogether. The best way was to start rumors that if we were forced to withdraw from conquered territories, I would be replaced by the army in favor of factions bent on armed conflict to maintain the extent of the empire, or more. Better to deal with me than military zealots, the story went. Molotov refined this story later on.

And I had learned to use national parties, not overt Soviet occupation.

Then, one day, events turned. Molotov came running into my office, actually sober. Roosevelt wanted to know if I would meet with him and Churchill somewhere in Scotland!

I could smell an opportunity. THEY wanted to meet with ME. I decided that whatever they wanted, they would have to give me a price: eastern europe at

the least. I didn't need them to finish off Germany.
In 1943, THEY needed ME! It was delightful.
Who did I have to thank? Hitler, of course. Hitler
had Churchill terrified because Hitler was so unpredictable. Hitler was also wildly successful, beyond anyone's worst predictions! The old aristocracy of England
was tied to the old aristocracy of Germany. Hitler had
little use for the monarchy. His victory threatened to
bring down all that was traditionally English, just as
the Bolsheviks had threatened to do in the Red scare
after the First World War. Churchill never forgave us
for shooting the Tsar, the look-alike cousin of the
English King George V.

In the face of modern logistics, Hitler's methods
had to fail. He was not an empire builder. He wanted
to build one people into something the world had
never seen: a racial empire. Empires are made of
different people, even different sub-nations pulling the
same wagon, or as I have constructed it, many peoples
toiling under the same yoke.

Hitler was another fool. The Japanese were much
better at planning genocide and then getting the
survivors to work for the controllers. But in the end,
they were like Lenin and Trotsky - fools. They lost.
They had to have everything, NOW. No patience.

Faced with an alternative, who could the West
choose: Hitler or me? The Great Patriotic War cost us
25 million dead. That was nothing. I killed that many
in 1932 by famine.

Hitler was the best thing that ever happened to
me. Why? He made me look good. Who else could
have done that?

He brought on a war that left europe devastated,
and the West in serious debt. He drew attention away

from our empire, and then, in trying to destroy us, gave me the means to develop military might to a level the West would not have otherwise allowed.

I paid for it with millions and millions of people.

But, In 1945, I could face the world and say I defeated fascism and defended democracy.

My democracy.

Koba
5 October 1952

CHAPTER TWELVE

TEHERAN

On November 28, 1943, I met the American President Roosevelt in our embassy in Teheran. It was important for me to make the first meeting on our soil, even if only on embassy grounds. He sat. I stood. That is exactly how I played it afterwards, giving him all the respect I could muster as he tried to be my teacher and friend. The story of how the meeting came about is quite interesting.

Earlier, in August, 1942, Churchill, then the British Prime Minister, came to meet me in Moscow.

The Germans had pushed through to the Caucuses and had the entire Volga River under fire. Their panzers had just taken the area north of Stalingrad. The War was at its worst for us. A reasonable man might have asked if we would survive. Churchill was in great spirits as he asked me the very question. My answer was just a shrug. "Maybe." Oh, how I despise Churchill and his pompous attitude, but more, how I despise his desire to see us Bolsheviks shot.

At any rate, from August 1942 through the winter we fought the immortal Battle of Stalingrad which became a meat grinder for the German Wermacht. The Red Army is made from more than Russians. At

Stalingrad, I committed everyone, Russians, Chinese, Koreans, and Kurds. It took months, but we smashed a German Army by eating it alive, street by street, day by day. I did not care about casualties because this was our big chance; they could not replace their losses. The fighting was savage, without stop. Much of it was hand to hand in the destroyed streets of the small city.

We won the battle through months of intense, costly combat. Success can be expensive.

After Stalingrad, I made peace overtures to the Germans, but Hitler wouldn't have any part of it. He wasn't interested. I offered to go back to the 1941 boundaries. I offered to let the War wind down so he could go back to chasing the English on a full time basis. No. No interest.

Hitler kept committing troops against us all along the lines. Eventually, the great tank battle at Kursk took place in July, 1943. We smashed the German armored units, finally defeating their ability to run the blitzkrieg in Russia.

This had nothing to do with running out of gas or winter. We went nose to nose with German Armor on a dusty plain in the summer. They had plenty of gas. We beat them in a running tank battle by superior tactics and better tanks.

I knew, therefore, in July 1943 that we would defeat Germany. I had seen how the momentum of warfare changes direction during our Revolution. A war effectively ends before the generals lay down their arms. Both sides fight on, the losers so uselessly, while defeated leaders decide how to protect their asses. I was still building strength when the Germans were thrown on the defensive.

My offensive power could not be stopped by the

forces available to the Germans. I knew my forces could bleed them dry. I expect a lot of Swiss bank accounts were opened by powerful Germans in August, 1943.

I didn't care how long it took. We had the Germans by the throat and would win even if we had to fight through to Berlin. By 1943, I could have lost Moscow in an isolated battle. It didn't matter. We had moved all our power back, behind the Caucuses. Once we reorganized, and started moving forward, we were unstoppable.

The theory of attack was simple: Forward. Anyone who moved back was shot. I shot generals and privates. Our troops always moved forward in battle. NKVD units were positioned behind the front lines. If they found a soldier in the rear who should have been at the front, they shot him. Then we looked up his family and took care of them, too. Gulags. Motivation.

Unlike the Tsars, I starved people in order to build plentiful munitions. In this War, after Stalingrad, our soldiers went into battle with modern weapons, artillery and air support. Trotsky had taught me the violent nature of war, and the simple desires of soldiers - food and weapons. My soldiers had both.

Fight to win. Find the Germans, kill them all, fast. We did.

I hated Churchill. He was a clever, shrewd man.

He knew what the Soviet Union intended, and what I wanted from the Revolution up to the Teheran meeting. I was constantly finding and shooting his spies. The British never forgave us for shooting the Romanovs. Churchill had been involved in the foreign occupations against the Reds after the Revolution. He would have greatly preferred to have shot me instead of having to talk to me.

In 1941 and 1942, Britain and America wanted Russia to fight to the death to slow down and tire out the Germans, thus to save the English from becoming another France. This was the exact reverse of my plan to let the Germans fight it out with the Western Allies, softening them all up for my blows.

After Kursk, things changed. We were not fighting for mere survival. We were on the offensive and I had not yet brought all our forces to bear. Churchill understood what an opportunity this offered because he had studied the history of europe where power, not geography, shapes borders.

Before the War, Roosevelt and Churchill had no use for me. Churchill knew I wanted all europe and meant to have it, even if I had to share it with Hitler for a while. By 1943, as Prime Minister, he saw that I might attain the same goal by defeating Germany and rolling up their recent conquests as my own empire.

He was worried that by 1946 or 1947, Britain would be looking at a europe occupied by my Red Army of 20 million experienced combat troops. I hoped for 1947 or 48, but, I shared the same dream.

He was right. When Kursk ended, we had a wild celebration in the Kremlin. The War, and possibly europe, was ours. Earlier, we had been desperate for the Allies to begin a second front in europe by invading France. After Kursk, I didn't care what the Allies did. We could win on our own and keep all we conquered.

The only use I had for the Allies was providing supplies and, most of all, banking credits. Lenin was right when he said the best way to fight the West was to allow them to finance the making of the rope that would be used to hang them. I wanted the West to pay for the Red Army that would eventually take europe under Soviet control.

I was not happy about travelling out of the Soviet Union, because I was never secure that my generals would let me back in. I was the generalissimo and I had Zhukov running the military campaign. Voroshilov was my political watch on the Red Army, but he was too dumb to be dependable. Travel meant danger for me because I had many enemies.

If only a few of my present generals acted, I might be finished. Leaving the country meant leaving physical control behind. It made me quite nervous.

I had to consider that my enemies might blow up my plane on the way out. The only completely trustworthy generals I had were dead ones. The living ones performed, but I was extremely careful about their ability to shape personal loyalties against me. All generals' families were my pampered hostages. I made the message clear. Succeed or die. I meant their entire family. It worked.

As a nation, we were broke. I had industrial might sufficient to win the War, but I needed money as the priming oil of production. So, I agreed to meet with Roosevelt and that pig, Churchill. After much discussion, we agreed on Teheran, Iran, which is just south of our border. There was no precise agenda. We were supposed to talk about the coordination of the War. I didn't care much about that.

I have read a great deal in the Western press about how I went to the meeting to force the Allies to land as soon as possible in France and begin the second front to cause the speedy surrender of Germany.

No. That's not true at all. By August, 1943, I wanted the Allies to stay out of europe. If they landed in France, the war would go faster, but their occupation meant I would not be able to grab the whole continent.

I had an extensive intelligence network in the United States and Britain. It cost a great deal of money to run. Words and threats may squeeze production or courage from workers and soldiers, but intelligence requires hard cash for expenses such as equipment, bribes, and embassies. The embassy staff has to eat. They buy their food locally. It requires cash. I couldn't rob their host nation's national banks and treasuries at gunpoint, but I could rob the Allied leaders with words.

I did.

At our meeting in Teheran, I found Churchill crusty as ever, but Roosevelt pleasantly disposed to listen to me. That was all I needed.

I told Roosevelt how great he was. He told me how great I was. Churchill fumed, but it didn't matter. Roosevelt was in charge because the United States provided all the money and fighting power to keep Britain out of the crushing German grip. Any second front would be an American led and financed effort involving British forces. What had been a three-power conference became a two man discussion.

I saw Roosevelt as the enemy. He was our ally in 1943, but as I looked at him, I saw past Teheran to the years after the War. I knew what I wanted. Roosevelt didn't have a long term plan. Churchill wanted to survive, but he was also looking beyond the War. Roosevelt saw only the War and his 1944 election.

It was very worth while for me to meet my former enemies. My Chekists found that Churchill was indeed trying to inspire my generals to kill me. He wanted to blow up my plane when I left Teheran. It was all stopped. I, on the other hand, didn't have to kill him to get rid of him. I needed funds to help get rid of him in his elections. Democracy offers an easy alternative to assassination - elections.

We have elections in the empire that are performances of our power. Democracies have elections to periodically gut themselves, diminishing the power of the state by disrupting its continuity. With cash, I can make a difference in any election, anywhere - except here, where cash is not the manifestation of power.

I wanted to get rid of Churchill. I would have loved to have blown up HIS plane, but the British took good care of him. So I decided to try and get Roosevelt to help me.

For months before the meeting, I had our spies tell their contacts in the United States Government that I was dumb, alcoholic, afraid, sick, and close to collapse. I also had them circulate the story that the Soviet Union was in danger of collapse because of the strains of the War, and that without strong, fast aid, we would go under.

What kind of aid? Everything! But especially credits so that we could buy munitions and pay for governmental operations to carry on the War. I let it be known that I was dedicated to the War (I wasn't) and that some of my generals might throw me over and make a separate peace with the Germans (they wouldn't). It cost a lot, but the story was accepted throughout their State Department where I had a lot of admirers. (I still do!)

I kept hammering away for a second front through formal and informal channels, even though I didn't want one. It was the only way I could get the Americans to believe that I needed help. I needed their money, but not their military help. Unfortunately, I couldn't get the former without feigning the latter. The louder I called for a second front, the more I hoped they would reward me for my patience.

When we met, Roosevelt's intelligence briefing painted me as a reclusive, paranoid fool, but a useful one as compared to others in the Soviet Government.

I just about wrote the brief.

It was delightful to watch Roosevelt's fatherly calm when he talked to me as though I might not understand. Churchill grew angry watching the spectacle. His blood pressure would shoot up and his cheeks would turn red. He always needed a drink.

Roosevelt took great pains to explain to me that I could trust him. He wanted me to understand that the Allies were not waiting to get the second front going in order to have the Russians and Germans fight each other into a mutual grave. He told me that if I was patient, all would be well, that the Allies would mount the european invasion - but that it would take time.

He wanted me to trust him and the Allied intent. I was happy as a lark! I would mumble my feeble acquiesce. He would again try to get me to believe in him, to trust him. I got the impression he wanted me to like him.

I hated him, his rich, phoney culture and his attitude, but I loved his response to my rumors.

He finally asked what it would take to show his sincerity. I told him I didn't understand. He insisted on doing something to show how seriously and honorably I should regard him. I told him I didn't understand. He finally insisted that I accept credits for the purchase of War material or general use in the United States and elsewhere, a big, virtually blank check to buy German-killing supplies. Once you have the credits, you don't have to spend it all on supplies. When you send your agents shopping, they get access to all channels in the government, the defense contractors, the military itself, and of course, the US State Department.

That's when Churchill tried to give me the sword. It's an interesting story.

The English King George VI had commissioned some of his best armorers to make a commemorative sword as a gift to the people of Stalingrad. It was touching, but stupid.

There were no people in Stalingrad. The ones that weren't killed were shipped elsewhere. I felt they were not dedicated enough if they survived. Churchill came to the conference with this sword, and wanted to have a public presentation, complete with movie film, speeches and radio coverage. Considering that I had spent almost twenty years aiming hard propaganda against the British and Americans, I was not prone to accept an invitation to be filmed shaking hands with them and smiling happily. Movie film is the most devastating propaganda vehicle.

But, Roosevelt thought it was a good idea. One night during the conference, Lavrenty Beria, my Cheka chief since I shot Yagoda in 1938, called to warn me not to accept the sword in public, because Churchill had arranged to have me either shot or blown up at the ceremony. The British had considerable influence in Teheran, and they could easily arrange the action.

I begged off the presentation, claiming illness.
Churchill insisted, promising it would only take fifteen
minutes. Roosevelt, who didn't know any better,
thought it would be a grand gesture of Allied unifica-
tion against Germany.

I offered another suggestion - wouldn't it be better
if one of my generals or a survivor of Stalingrad
accepted? No, Churchill and Roosevelt thought it
important that the ceremony be recorded as an entente
among nations, not just celebration of a single battle.

As the time became imminent, I did the logical
thing. I contacted Roosevelt in private and told him
that I had security concerns about the presentation,
especially if it took place outdoors. I told him that
some of my generals were ready to do anything to get
rid of me, but that for political reasons, I could not
move against them at this time.

I added that I was concerned about the safety of
Roosevelt and Churchill, who would be close by when
the clumsy Russians acted.

That did it. While Roosevelt had ample confidence
in his security people, he couldn't stomach a direct
threat against his personal safety. He could order
millions into peril, but he could not stand the prospect
of personal danger.

So, the presentation took place indoors. Only still
pictures were taken. Churchill, red cheeked, made a
passionate performance. So did I. It's a beautiful
sword. Beria's men found there was a plot, and later
identified the agents involved. They were local to
Teheran. They were going to blow up my car en route
to the British Embassy where the ceremony was
initially planned. Then the British would kill the
plotters to seal the secret.

Roosevelt was trying to be my friend and Churchill was trying to kill me. It was going very well.

One morning, Roosevelt and Churchill came to see me for a regular series of talks. Roosevelt immediately began to make fun of Churchill, who had no sense of humor. I don't mean one joke.

Roosevelt kept kidding Churchill about how stiff the British were, how their image was so combative and moody, and how Churchill should relax. I was amazed.

Roosevelt gave a performance intended to make me feel relaxed. It was one of the silliest things I have ever seen a head of state inflict on another leader. It went on for some time. Poor Churchill! He probably wanted to storm out and return to London, but he couldn't. He had to endure the jibes of his paymaster. I knew, then, that my plans had worked. Roosevelt, the leader of the most powerful and wealthy country on earth wanted to be my friend.

I think Roosevelt's General Marshall knew what the game was, but he was only a general, thus power-less. I saw hatred in Marshall's eyes. But, Roosevelt wanted to help.

I broke down, and let him! He gave me millions. He also hinted at giving me Poland and the Baltic States. He threw in the idea of a world-wide political organization that would exist after the War for the purpose of providing world security - or as I saw it, potential world propaganda.

No one asked what we intended to do in europe. No one seemed to care what would happen to Soviet occupied areas. I knew they were concerned, but they were too timid.

Molotov, my Foreign Minister, is a drunken idiot,

but he gave me one piece of advice in 1941 that I have followed ever since. When I wanted something from the allies, I had Beria's people circulate rumors that if I did not get foreign support, I would be replaced by generals who would take an adverse position to the Allies - in this case, surrender to the Germans. It works like a charm. Adversaries back away. The fear of dealing with unknown zealots makes diplomats cower. Leaders who should oppose you now support you. Career diplomats absorb this planted, phony noise with the most serious study, and start to offer complex opinions to their political masters who assume the diplomats know what they are doing. They don't.

Career diplomats exist to continue their existence. I use embassies to support intelligence work and propaganda. The West uses embassies as overseas boarding schools for the failed sons and daughters of the aristocracy who can't find gainful employment elsewhere. Even the false hint of a political problem in the empire had the Americans and British Foreign Services issuing reams of paper to show the depth of their knowledge, the value of their bureaucratic existence, and the probability of grave consequences if anything happened to disturb the status quo.

I like diplomats. I should; I own enough of them.

Roosevelt should have been the champion of his democracy; instead, he wanted to be my friend. It was a windfall.

I had believed that european conquest might be achieved only by military means. The Teheran Conference gave me reason to think it might be achieved by gift, through political means. I believed the Americans could make a formidable military enemy, even if thousands of kilometers away. I knew, from spies, that they were working on new weapons which would allow them to use air power to destroy whole nations from great distances. Therefore, The United States had moved right next to europe in the balance of military power.

The Teheran conference was cut short because Roosevelt had to leave on December 2 to avoid bad weather. When I returned to Moscow, the War news was good. We continued to pound away. Germany's defeat was just a matter of time and several million more lives.

Luckily, we had not been involved in the Japanese theater of operations. The Americans wanted control of Japan after the War. Roosevelt wanted us to consider coming into the Japanese War to help finish them off, once and for all. I studied our opportunities.

Roosevelt saw Japan.

I saw China.

Since the Allies were probably going to invade europe, I decided to finish off Germany, then keep troops in the occupied areas of europe to the greatest extent possible without getting into a shooting war with the West.

We would avoid actual fighting with the Allies for control of post-war europe, concentrating on China first. Once we had China, we would turn on europe with political and propaganda firepower. By then the Americans might have pulled out. Europe would be economically devastated, thus, ripe for our style of Revolution and occupation. Europe would fall into our arms willingly.

While everyone in the West was worried about our move into europe, I would turn and take Japan by use of Chinese forces.

To make the plan work, I needed an agreement to keep our troops in place in europe when Germany fell.

While we had discussed many topics, no firm agreements had been worked out. I needed Roosevelt's specific permission. I needed it in a hurry because he was dying.

I got it - at Yalta, my favorite wartime conference of the Allies.

By the time of the Teheran conference, we had victory in our grasp. With Yalta, we had the war won. I agreed to the conference to see what I could get.

I got a lot.

Unsigned (same handwriting)
6 November 1952

Author's Note: As I mentioned, not all the pieces were signed. This one is clearly in Stalin's handwriting. It was written on the back of organizational memos for the year's October Revolution celebrations. He used a fountain pen with a dark brown ink, a fashion in the Kremlin through the post war years. The date is in his writing.

CHAPTER THIRTEEN

YALTA

When I was a boy we celebrated Christmas and the New Year in grand style. If we were lucky, as children, we got a full dinner on Christmas. We were poor. What mattered was food. Very wealthy families had presents, usually wooden toys in the fashion of Tsarist military figurines or traditional dolls.

It was more a celebration of religious ideas and the family.

When the Revolution came to power, we changed the holiday. Now we send cards and exchange presents for the New Year, not Christmas.

The last time we had an official Christmas in Russia was 1916. The last time I celebrated Christmas, however, was at Yalta, from February 4 to 11, 1945.

The War had gone well. My armies were about fifty kilometers outside Berlin. We got there on our own, starting with the victories at Stalingrad and Kursk, moving forward without stop.

At the Teheran conference, Roosevelt tried to get me to be his friend, to trust him. He kept it up and wanted to continue the relationship in Yalta. Yalta is in the Crimea, in the south of the empire. I enjoyed making the great leaders come to me.

In Teheran, Roosevelt hinted that if I wanted Poland, I could have it.

In Yalta, he gave it to me. Roosevelt couldn't do enough for me. We talked about the United Nations.

Did I want multiple seats? Sure! They gave me seats for The Soviet Union, The Ukraine and Byelorussia. The Americans got one seat. Did I want some of the Japanese Islands for promising to come into the Pacific War (now that it was just about over)? Sure! Did I want a chunk of Germany? Sure! Did I want some of northern China? Sure! Did I want the British out of Yugoslavia? Sure! Did I want to internationalize Indochina? I didn't know where Indochina was - but sure!

All during the War, there had been governments in exile in europe, and they had maintained troops under national flags, supported by the British, who in turn, were supported by the Americans. I did not like the idea of several Polish divisions loose in europe after the War. At Yalta, Churchill and Roosevelt agreed to disarm them and send them back to me! They agreed to send back the foreign nationals that had escaped my grasp and were running foreign govern- ments in exile for the Red occupied territories. Every- one knew I'd send them off to the gulags.

They agreed to send back ordinary people who had escaped the Germans by fleeing before the blitzk- rieg. Churchill didn't want them. Roosevelt either didn't care or didn't understand. Any East Germans who fled to the Western Zones would be sent back. I was delighted. I wanted them all. Siberia has lots of room.

I couldn't see why they agreed.

I didn't promise to give them anything. In fact, with a straight face, I told them that I would have to go back to Moscow and sell the deal to the Politburo. Of course, I was the Politburo. Me. I was the entire government. I told them Molotov-inspired stories about my tenuous position with a straight face and they asked how they could help.

I thought about it.

About the only thing they could do beyond their gifts so far was to give me Paris or London, now. Roosevelt just about did. He told me that the Americans would probably stay in europe for only a couple of years after the War!

I could wait.

What's two years? I could bide my time, especially since Roosevelt was obviously dying. He didn't look good in Teheran, but now he was failing right before my eyes. Two years! If they left, europe would be unprotected!

Roosevelt had surrounded himself with subordinates of my own liking. Weaklings and more. I had a spy right in his entourage. His diplomats must have been using a crystal ball or some other instrument of divine guidance. They did not deal in reality.

The conference was for show. Roosevelt was too weak to do much. He wanted to get the United Nations going. I agreed. I wanted as many of my people loose in the United States as fast as possible.

After the conference I went back to Moscow and thought it over. Maybe I should have let the army smash through Germany, past Berlin and see how much we could grab. But I was right.

The Allies were concerned about europe. Europe was destroyed. They forgot that war can be waged on the political front as viciously as on the military front.

Then there was China. Roosevelt was willing to

give me Port Arthur, which meant he was going to give me effective control of Manchuria. Port Arthur had been the administrative capital of the Japanese regime over Manchuria. Once Roosevelt died, how was his successor going to explain this gift to that fanatical Chinese nationalist, Chaing Kai Chek? But then, how would the poor successor explain Poland and the negotiation over Lithuania. Roosevelt wanted to give them to me.

My greatest fear was that the Allies would not stop at Berlin. I watched to see if they would come after my armies, as some in the American ranks suggested. But they didn't. Roosevelt wouldn't let them. He should have. He should have let the Allied military grab as much as it could. Instead, they were ordered to hold back. We had defeated Germany, but my armies were stretched over 2,000 kilometers through burned out squalor. Behind the front, there was nothing but open space. The Allies used a highly mobile form of warfare. They had unlimited tanks, supply trucks, and troop vehicles. Their air forces were huge and built for long distance operations. The Allies, if they had made a concerted effort, could have taken Moscow. They could have come at me from both sides at one time, europe and asia. In effect, the Allies had me surrounded with powerful, well-equipped forces.

What would they do with the conquered territory if they came after me? I didn't mind famine. Could they endure it? Could they afford to take and then administer such an enormous area with a large, hungry population? No. They were content to let me take care of it. They wanted to go home. I was the only hunter. I was safe because they were tired.

I had my work cut out. A lot of my people had

gotten out of control. Red soldiers had been captured, and populations had been occupied by the Germans and others. All my soldiers and people should have fought to the death!

I could never trust anyone who had been involved with the West, except Molotov, who didn't know where he was from day to day, which is why I trusted him as my Foreign Minister. Once exposed to Western ideas, people were useless to me. If they could see past me, then I had to kill them. It was just a few million more.

As our Red Army went back through Poland and the Ukraine, we recovered many of our soldiers who had surrendered or had been cut off behind German lines. Many had fought bravely on behalf of the Rodina, the Motherland, but it didn't matter. All went to the gulags. They had to be sent. Many were executed in secret by the NKVD as traitors. We told their families they were missing. They were. Forever.

I came away from Yalta with a bag full of presents that I had never thought I would get. I also had Roosevelt's promise that the Allies would stay partners with me and that what I had taken would remain mine. No one was going to come after the empire.

And, I would have a new organization to use to our advantage, somewhere in the United States, which is where I wanted it to be. The mere idea of a United Nations made me laugh.

The Americans would end up paying for the Soviets to be able to penetrate foreign governments collected in one place. It was an intelligence dream! My Chekists were overjoyed.

I felt like I was talking to the ghost of Woodrow Wilson.

"Well," I told them," it will be a tough sale at home!" What trusting fools!

Roosevelt died in April just before I sent the Red Army into Berlin. On May 2, Berlin was mine.

In 1941, we were almost wiped out. As I thought it over, I realized Hitler had done me a great service. I would avenge the Russian losses in the 1905 Japanese War. The empire would stretch from the regained Japanese Islands to Berlin. All mine. All completely mine.

The only people who might have opposed me under arms or on the political front were now rendered powerless by their "victory." They thought the War was over. The real War, the one that began in the 1920's was still "on."

Churchill was going to be kicked out by his voters. Roosevelt had died. Yalta taught me that pressure was the key. I decided to keep constant political pressure on the democracies and watch them stumble. Yalta told me they were concerned about what happened only in europe, that the great leaders were limited in scope. Yalta confirmed what I thought.

The Allies didn't understand world politics. They believed their own propaganda about Hitler being the great enemy of all time. Quite wrong. I was the great enemy. I had learned that the world was changing. I would use political war instead of a shooting war. I would use local "talent" to run political operations in foreign nations, thereby avoiding national resistance to "Russian" organs.

Yalta convinced me to wait and let europe crumble. It also told me to go after China, because the Allies didn't care about or understand mainland asia.

It was as though history commanded me to go

after China.

The Yalta Conference produced only one official result: a promise not to fight among ourselves when the War ended. But, because I got the secret promises and permissions I wanted, there wasn't anything to fight over. Molotov told me he thought I did a great job.

I told him he should thank Roosevelt, my friend.

The English and the French had declared war on Germany because of the Polish invasion. They left me alone then, even though I got half of Poland after invading from the east as Hitler's partner. I just couldn't believe Roosevelt and Churchill. Now that the War was almost over, they were giving me all of Poland, knowing what I was going to do. They were giving me Manchuria, which had been one of the Japanese occupations leading to the War.

What was the War all about for these men? Was it really about Poland? Was it about the defeat of the Japanese Empire? For me it was survival and power. I never did figure out what they wanted from the War.

They gave me Poland. I kept all the conquered territories, except Austria, which I turned into a gelding.

Years later, now that I have China, I still can't believe what those "leaders" did.

Complete victory was in their hands.

Now, I have nuclear weapons.

Koba
1 December 1952

CHAPTER FOURTEEN

FINANCE

One day, I hope I can put the weight of leadership aside and semi-retire. I know I can't, because the instant I become vulnerable my comrades will turn and kill me. But I would like to slow down and take it easy. As I look around the world these days, there is a surplus of featherweight leadership. Where did they come from? From under what gigantic rock did they all crawl?

The Great Patriotic War was fought and won by me. The empire is larger and more powerful than ever. I claim control across half the world. Absolute control. There is no opposition. There is no enemy. The world is afraid of me.

I don't know why.

Everything I have has been ignorantly handed to me. Trotsky won the Civil War, then abandoned his right to be Lenin's heir. The United States and Great Britain gave me eastern europe in the Teheran and Yalta conferences. They lost mainland China by supporting a bunch of gangsters on the losing side. If I desired, I could reach out and take India from British control by funding and shaping a new Indian National-ist Movement under Red command. If I really tried, I might be able to grab Mexico or another country in south america.

I keep building the army. I have to. We won't use it, because I can't afford to have generals run loose. In the long term, they can't be controlled or trusted. But, as long as I let them spend on munitions and weapons they stay busy and happy. I end up with a huge army even though I have no enemy. Do I get a return on the investment in weapons if we don't intend to use them? Yes. I get peace at home. I stay in power, but at a great cost in cash and industrial output. I'm worth it. If not for me, for whom should this all be spent?

I made a mistake with Hitler. I knew he was the enemy all along, but I thought he would go against France and England, and that all three would be destroyed, ready for my taking. I'll get them yet, but I won't have to fire a shot. They will come to me when they go broke from overspending on their feeble attempts at university-inspired Socialism. Harmless Socialism exists only in books. It is born in misguided guilt, enforced at gunpoint and will sway the world's political order by force of arms. Talk is cheap. Real Socialism is anything but cheap.

The Americans don't bother me. They don't have the resolve to act against me.

I first tested this by closing Berlin to the West in 1947, in violation of the Allied treaty. Then, I tested them again in Korea in 1950, this time with Bismarck's "Blood and Iron." They talk a lot, but they won't attack Russia. They should. Their politicians have developed a political goal called, "status quo." They want things to be the same.

History says that cannot be true, ever. Organisms

that do not grow, mature and die. Nations can get fat. America is fat. It sits there, endowed by God with bounty and more - and just sits. I shake the world, and they only react to me. It's a shame.

They should conduct an economic war, but they won't move with monetary force or an embargo. They send "scouts" over to see what our condition is, businessmen looking for investment possibilities. We don't have investment possibilities. This is the last place on earth to invest capital, because I won't let profits out. Economic war works as effectively as a shooting conflict. The result can be the loss of a nation and the toppling of regimes.

I should explain how capital really works.

I know better than anyone else alive, because I studied Marx and his high priest, Lenin, for my whole adult life. Whatever they said is wrong. Don't blame them. They didn't know what they were talking about. They were Socialists. They never had any money and had never run a government. It was all theoretical expression, wishful fiction.

I wrote some of the most convoluted gibberish about the nature of capital. Some of it is mine; most of it is written by others for attribution to me. There are volumes of it written for the Party faithful to keep them confused and occupied. The bright ones spend hours studying the hidden evidence of genius in all this, even though there isn't any. When the spirit moved me, I could go for thousands of words to explain nothing.

When you are an absolute leader, people see genius in every meaningless word. If I took up the paintbrush, the art world would be turned on its ear by my genius. I could do it with the tuba. No matter

what I do, my cronies call it genius. I walk like a
genius. I drink like a genius.

But I am a genuine genius at finance.

Money is a commodity, just like grain or oil. It
means something to people who want it. It has little
meaning if people don't want it anymore. There are
many ways to get it.

Before I started robbing banks, Lenin was desperate. He couldn't borrow from anyone because he could
not repay. He couldn't print money because he wasn't
a government yet. He used to pace and fume that he
needed money, but couldn't get it. I was always
tempted to get the Party to collectively urge Lenin to
get a job. Lenin could never hold a job. Too jumpy.
Typical intellectual.

The Germans gave millions to get the Party into
Russia in 1917 because the Party promised to take
Russia out of the First World War. They paid for he
famous "sealed train" that took Lenin and the boys
from Switzerland to Finland for the entry into Petrograd. But the big money comes when you take over a
government and control the country. Then, you get
everyone's money, every last cent, without accoun-
tability. You can keep as much as you want, while
letting the working masses have just enough to get by.

Western economists use a term called "Gross
National Product" to represent the value of all transactions in an economic unit - typically a country. Because
Western economies run on cash, they can place a ready
value on their activity. We can't exactly do that. We
use barter quite a bit, that is, trading things for things
without the use of cash. If I want Fiat trucks for the
Red Army, I have my boys call Fiat and ask how many
barrels of oil they will charge per truck. I send them

a shipment of Baku oil; they deliver the trucks. They then sell the oil somewhere else in the world to raise cash to pay their workmen, parts suppliers, etc.

I use the trucks to scare the daylights out of europe.

Lenin was fixated by cash. He lived in fairly comfortable exile in western europe, so one might expect him to quantify everything in terms of cost. He did.

He always felt we were broke if we didn't have cash in our pockets. He understood that people needed to eat, and that farmers produce food, but he couldn't figure out how to get machinery out of that subtle equation. He was always trying to placate banks to get cash so we could buy things - in the West! He preached that borrowing from the West was only a way to use their own strength against them. I admit, there is some use to that, but not the way he intended.

Lenin thought he understood debt, but he didn't. I think deep in his mongolian heart he wanted to be a professor in some old, ivy-covered university where he could spout endlessly about theoretical rubbish, impressing ignorant children of the aristocracy with his philosophical pandering. I think he was secretly afraid of the rope.

Money is a cutting edge. You can talk about it until you are blue in the face - either you have it or you don't.

If you borrow money, you are supposed to pay it back. Presumably, when you borrowed it, you needed it. As soon as you got it, you spent it on something. Now comes the problem: how do you pay it back?

If the loan funds were wisely used, they would produce a cash flow sufficient to pay the interest on

the loan and the principal when due. If the project was
not successful, then the loan cash might be consumed,
but produce no result. How do you pay it back? You
can't. Westerners sue each other or file for bankruptcy
at this point.

The next time you go to borrow, lenders will say,
"No! You didn't pay the last lender." Now what? You
hire an expert investment banker to give you advice.
He'll tell you to offer some security to new lenders.
This way, if you don't pay the loan, the lenders can
sell the security and get repaid that way. Another way
is to offer a "sweetener." This means that if everyone
is paying 9% to borrow, you can attract attention if
you offer 10 or more per cent. If you are not a good
credit risk, you will have to pay still more.

Lenin could understand the theory, but he was
proud of his ignorance of financial market operations.
It caused problems that took me years to fix after I
killed him.

When you take over a government, bankers will
pursue. They want you. Politically they may hate you,
but as a client they love you. They love your debt.

Bankers get paid when they write loans. If they
don't write the loans, they go out of business. They are
on you like mosquitoes in summer. It doesn't matter
where you try to hide from them, they'll find you. I
think the NKVD could learn a lot from bankers in the
area of psychological warfare. Bankers don't use
torture. They use seduction.

Bankers look you over and tell you,"... things
would improve if you did thus-and-such. What? No
money to do it: no problem. We'll float a loan!" Worse:
"we'll sell bonds!"

Bonds are like small infections that get out of

control and kill your operation. A banker wants to do a loan immediately for a set amount. He may invite other banks into the overall loan for pieces of the deal. This is called a syndicate, which I understand is also the American slang term for organized crime.

On the other hand, an investment banker wants you to offer bonds through another kind of syndicate. This syndicate sells bonds to individual people, institutions and other governments.

As a government, if you borrow from a bank and don't pay, there isn't much they can directly do to you except blackball you from future loans. The problem with loans is that in accepting the theory, you have gone down the cash road of economic structure.

A cash economy requires cash. Where do you get it? How do you support it? You need it to pay back loans. You have to start keeping real sets of books to measure financial intake and output. Everything you do will thereafter be measured in fiscal productivity terms, not real terms. You will be measured on a periodic basis, not just yearly.

Since you have got a set of books, auditors will want to crawl all over your operation to see if the books are orderly and offer a reasonable description of the enterprise. All of a sudden, you lose the privacy of your operation and with it, the basis of control - secrecy.

No government should keep an orderly set of books. Either a large number of unintelligible books should be kept or a few false ones. As soon as a government has a set of financial books, everybody wants to see them.

Part of my genius is shown by the way I have structured the Soviet economy. When we talk about economics, we don't know what we are saying. I publish a five year, centrally planned directive. It is always a success. Any criticism buys a bullet. Officially, the Soviet Union has the most reliable economic success in the world today. In reality we're broke.

The worst situation occurs where, as a government, you sell bonds. Your bonds will be put together as one big package. Then brokers will be invited to take a small piece of the big package. If you needed 10 million roubles to build a railway, the investment bankers will try to get you to sell 30 million worth of bonds. Why? Because they make more money when they sell more bonds. That's what the brokers do.

You deliver a truckload of I.O.U.'s, and they start to sell them.

The first thing the investment banker tells you is that you need to sell more of the bonds to get other brokers interested. You can always find a use for the funds. If you can't find a use for cash lying around, you don't deserve to be in government. Loose cash is always up for grabs.

Then, after you have set up all your programs and depend on the sale of your bonds to raise the planned and committed cash, the investment bankers tell you that the markets are not "receptive." You will have to pay a higher rate than they had first indicated.

Next, they tell you a special concession is required to get the selling brokers "motivated." It costs you more and more to borrow. If you agree, the syndicate goes to work selling your bonds to people that have no need or understanding of what they are buying. The brokers don't buy them.

They sell them.

The people that buy the bonds expect you to pay.

If you don't, they get mad at you. When a lot of people are mad at you in foreign countries, some may be willing to do things to harm you, such as fund political groups that oppose you. People understand and use direct revenge. Revenge lives for a long time. Banks use more subtle political pressure, like getting their home governments to go to war with you to get the bank's money back. Nuclear weapons are the best defense against banker-inspired wars, especially when warheads will hit cowardly politicians!

By now, if you have left the door open a little bit, the bankers and investment bankers are all over you. You are getting deeper and deeper into debt. Suppose the project doesn't work? How do you repay? This is what Lenin didn't understand.

You can get addicted to money, needing it all the time to pay the light bill and to eat. If you don't have it, you starve. If you give a foreign banker control over your cash flow, he can strangle you at a time of his choosing by denying you cash when you need it the most.

If you are borrowing to buy food, the bankers will use their power to get very steep terms because they know you need the money to avoid the mob. During the Revolution, hungry mobs killed and actually ate some of the commissars in the field.

One of the worst aspects of fiance is that you have to have government bookkeepers. You need an Exchequer or Treasury. This is very risky. It means you have to keep international contacts among financial professionals - very difficult to control.

Generals are dangerous because they control troops, but exchequers control the availability of cash. If you go to a cash economy, your people need cash to

buy bread. No cash, no bread. No bread, they come
looking for you. With guns.

A powerful central bank may be necessary to keep
the foreign bankers happy, but the same central bank
can break you as a leader by playing around with the
availability of cash. A leader cannot bend to pressure
from bankers.

It all comes back to the same thing: if you borrow,
you become dependent on more borrowing and you
give up control. If you run a government on cash, you
will eventually find the bankers telling you how to run
your government.

Don't do it.

One of the reasons Lenin had to die was that he
was about to go on a debt binge. In my office desk, I
keep a real Railroad Bond issued by the Tsars to build
the Trans Siberian Railroad. It is worthless today
because we killed the Tsar and destroyed his government. One of the prime reasons the foreign powers
tried to crush the Reds by sending troops into Russia
in 1918 was to make sure these bonds were paid. The
foreign governments were angry that we had shot the
Tsar and had pulled out of the War. But, they were
really angry about the bond issues, knowing we would
not pay.

This bond caused a small war.

Lenin talked grand economic theory, but he didn't
have a clue about setting up a treasury or what that
would mean to our control. He didn't see the danger
of Bolshevik control falling to banker control. I tried to
convince him that he was no banker. He said he would
learn when he had time. None of us was a banker. I
think I was the only one that had a background in
business life.

I learned business from the merchants of Tiflis and Gori. No matter what academics argue, all finance works on a simple basis. I could repeat it a hundred times. Either you have money or you don't. We set up a government without money. Lenin was about to sell our independence to the bankers.

I, on the other hand, now control the largest organization ever built.

The largest. Ever.

I did it without debt, except on the rarest of occasions.

Here's how.

When I got rid of Lenin, I needed cash, but I knew if I borrowed, I would have a regular, fixed charge. I looked around. We had already robbed all the banks. Where was the money?

It was in the countryside. The farmers and land owners had it. Farmers grow things. They create wealth. If you put a seed in the ground and take a little care of it, God does all the rest. You end up with wheat. People will pay money for wheat. Back in Moscow I had the boys figure out how much wheat was produced, and where it was produced in the Soviet Union. It was amazing.

I didn't look at it as wheat. I saw it as money. Think of a field of wheat in a late summer breeze. The wheat is tall. It beckons with its bending, golden color. Wheat shines after a rainfall. Yes, it is wheat, but, at the same time, it's money.

I would have to do a few transactions, but after I knocked off the bank in Tiflis we had to sell some of the larger bills at a discount because they had been reported stolen throughout Europe. A few alterations here and there are not a big difficulty. Everything is negotiable in business.

I decided to take the wheat and sell it on the world markets, mostly to europe. One of my biggest sales areas was Germany. France bought a lot. These foreign countries paid with cash! All I had to do was gather the wheat, put it on rail cars and deliver. Once I got the cash, I could then build factories to make steel, engines, power plants, and more, because I could pay for the machines I had to import.

I took over a very backward country and intended to change all deficiency. It got to the point that I would price wheat against machine delivery, without use of any cash. I re-invented industrial bartering.

Sometimes, if a good machinery deal came along, I might make a short term loan, but I always had the wheat for export. The crop might require a little more ripening, but I knew it was there, ready for shipment. I borrowed cash for a special deal, but I had alternative "cash" in ripening wheat. I was covered.

When I built a power plant, I again used farm products for export. If the Americans were selling wheat cheaply, I would underprice them. My wheat cost me nothing because I took it. I could price it as low as I wanted. Once I had built manufacturing plants that made guns and bullets for the Red Army, I sold some of that production overseas to raise money to build further factories.

I sold the Germans millions of the bullets they later shot at us. I sold them fleets of the trucks they used to ride through Russia. I did it for the money. On the other hand, many lathes that turned out Soviet aircraft parts were made by Krupp, bought with Deutschmarks that I got for Ukrainian wheat.

I put electric lights in the major cities and I fed

the Party well. You can't run a country without some cash. Industrial barter can be used to get products you can't otherwise afford, but you need some cash to keep your people happy inside the country - I mean Party members - and to pay for your intelligence services outside the country.

I had a number of politicians on my payroll all around the world. That takes cash. You can't bribe a man with a ton of wheat. But you can bribe a man for surprisingly little cash.

Here's another point. Industrial nations invest heavily in research and development of new products. This is necessary to their economic vitality. The United States spent billions of dollars to develop an atomic weapon.

It cost me less than one million dollars to steal it.

The Soviet Union doesn't have to invest in research if we wisely target Western industry and steal their secrets. Industrial espionage is vital in peacetime. It is also profitable.

It is not possible, however, to have a large military force, armed and ready, and have a stable civilian economy. Military forces are extremely costly. The West pays for theirs with debt.

They borrow money to pay for their military. I can't borrow much in the international markets, except for specific projects that have direct benefit for Western trade. In order to pay for my military, I have to pay now. Russians feel it now. Westerners are delaying the time when they will feel it.

It is a long distance race. Can I hold out and still spend on my military so that we are ready to act when all their debt crashes, or will we succumb first?

In government, keep looking for your national

assets.

When you rob a bank, you don't have to pay them back. When you steal wheat, you don't pay it back either. Once we figured out where our farming assets were, the Ukraine, I used Russian Reds to go and get it all. Russians didn't care what was happening to Ukrainians. Different Church, different language, different country. We took every last kernel. We stole every pig, cow, and chicken. From 1929 to 1934, 25 million people died from starvation.

I needed the money.

It was either that or the bankers. If I go to the bankers, they will ask for some control to avoid repudiation of the debt. They will ask for security. I won't give it. I can't give any power to anyone. The moment I do, it will be turned against me.

The West and the Bolsheviks have travelled down two separate roads. Ours is simpler. It is more direct. It is my road. The West started out with independence, but I am doing all in my power to push them onto the path of Socialism. Once there, all the money on earth cannot pay for the demands their central governments will incur. Either they will suddenly arrive at fascism or they will go broke and shatter.

The Germans went to fascism after a weak try at Socialism. If the West goes fascist, they will fight among themselves. Fine. Let them.

If they continue toward Socialism, they will fall when their debt exceeds their dreams.

My currencies are wheat, farm animals, natural resources, people and terror. I deal in present value.

I look at it this way: if I didn't steal the wheat, I could not have bought the machinery nor fed the workers and Red Army who allowed me to win the

Great Patriotic War in which I lost another 25 million people.

I am developing a new plan against the West.

As industrialized nations, they are constantly searching for resources. While they have many resources within their borders, they need more. They are like Japan before 1938. If they do not expand their influence, they will wither.

I remember how, as a new nation, the bankers came to us and wanted to do business - on their terms. I rejected it. We couldn't afford their "help."

But I have noticed bankers at work in the developing nations around the perimeter of China and in South America. I have numerous agents in all the affected areas. They are filled with corrupt governments.

What would happen if Western bankers loaned a lot of money to developing, poor countries? The cash would disappear into a thousand corrupt pockets.

If the loan proceeds are not used productively, how will the loans be repaid?

They won't.

What will happen to Western economies if some of their large banks fail because these loans will not be repaid?

What will happen if the West becomes dependent on resources that are geographically limited - like oil?

What will happen if my controlled insurgencies in developing nations go to war with their neighbors, requiring massive expenditures from the West to stop the aggression? Who will pay?

I have work to do.

You see, it all adds up.

I can wait. Draining capital resources from the

West is like drawing their blood. Oddly, my ally is their political fraternity, because governments do one thing well - spend. Bureaucrats consume.

It makes them important. It offers power and patronage. Productivity?

Irrelevant. Bureaucrats don't care.

They pay for it by printing money and borrowing more.

And more.

As I said, it adds up.

                              Koba
                              25 December 1952

CHAPTER FIFTEEN

POLITICAL FRIENDSHIP

As I have grown older and more experienced in life, I realize much of my early youth doted on the myth of friendship.

There is no such thing.

It is a sentimental way of looking at life that comes from self pity or undeserved emotional attachment. People cry when they see a pet die, yet soldiers cheer when they see an enemy die.

We place emotions in situations because of the way we grow up, are taught, or imagine the situation demands. We can laugh or cry at the same event - be it life or death.

Lenin tried to teach people to drop their emotions, to look at the world objectively, "scientifically." When he regularly failed, he would label the uncooperative thickheads "counterrevolutionaries," and remind Dzerzhinsky or myself to have them shot.

Lenin didn't realize that people cannot help but use emotions with every breath. The challenge is not to eradicate emotion, but to accept it and recognize the confusion it causes. It's very much like the recognition and control of religion.

Fear motivates flight. People run away because

they are afraid to stay where they were. They can be afraid of another person, an invading army, or starvation.

Fear is uncontrollable in its early physical manifestation. Fear makes strong legs weak. It makes your stomach turn. It makes people bolt on the spot for some other place. Courage overcomes fear, but only after the hero has felt fear. Courage tells you to fight on. Courage tells you to stay.

If a soldier on the battlefield lets fear take control, he may get up and try to run away, but be cut down by bullets, shrapnel or explosives. There are other examples of how fear can kill a man. Primitive instinct is not the answer to complex danger.

A soldier needs courage to stay put. He needs more courage to advance under fire.

Oddly, courage has no place in modern politics. There was an age when soldiers expected to be led by their generals in the field. People expected to be led by emperors who were in command. Something happened.

People now accept the cowardice of staff officials. Generals don't lead into battle; they lead into paperwork. Emperors don't lead a nation, they coordinate staffs, arriving at a heralded consensus.

World War One broke the european monarchies. Many disappeared, but all were shown to be fools. The enormity of war made people believe that large staffs were necessary for the complex operations of the military. After the War, similar, great organs were needed to run governments. Perhaps people felt exhaustion due to the increasing speed of events. Did people give up when they realized they could not know all there is to know? Did they surrender to the seduction of political specialists, who really don't know any more than anyone else?

What motivates people to give away control of their governments and lives? The West produces leaders who give the people what they want, but the people don't know what they want, so the leadership drifts, without responsibility. Western leadership is becoming unaccountable to those who are led. I, of course, am completely unaccountable! Will the West continue this drift and wake up under the control of opportunistic, bureaucratic fascism?

I have always been motivated by fear and greed. It reminds me of the old question: what does the fish see when he looks out of the bowl?

We only know what it looks like when we stare into the bowl.

High level politics makes you crazy. You are the fish looking out. Normal people try to guess what you are up to as they look in at you. The two visions cannot match. They come from two different worlds, going right past each other.

When I was part of the Socialist movement, I could do and say as I pleased because we were essentially anarchists with no agenda, except removal of the Tsar.

When I became a Bolshevik, I wanted to be part of the group I thought the most interesting, and, I admit, because I thought Lenin was intelligent.

But, I stayed a Bolshevik through the Revolution and the Lenin years out of fear. A soldier stays put because of courage. I stayed because I had no place to go, because many forces would have tracked me down and killed me, and because I could smell the possibility of real power. I stayed because I was afraid to leave and form my own group, when I could perhaps grab power from within the existing organization, right under the noses of the Politburo.

Lenin was surrounded by fanatics and fatheads, men who would do anything in the name of the Revolution. I did some of the most gruesome and heartless things for the cause, but I knew what I was doing and why. With the exception of Dzerzhinsky, Trotsky and Kirov, the rest didn't have the brains to know what day of the week it was, much less appreciate the meaning of our actions.

Once in progress, we all became prisoners of the Revolution. This is the real reason Lenin had the Tsar shot.

Lenin hated the Romanovs because they had executed his older brother Sasha for his participation in the plot to assassinate Tsar Alexander III. Alexander II had been blown up. The Okhrana was more efficient in protecting his son, Alexander III. Sasha could have been given a sentence of exile if he had agreed to disclose all the secrets of the plot, but he refused. He was executed in May, 1887.

Lenin, who kept telling people to reject emotion, was filled with it. He was carried by it. He always sought revenge. But close up, when he recognized danger, he ran. He was a physical coward, afraid of pain, probably afraid of death, because if he was wrong, and there was a God, then he, Lenin, would be in trouble for eternity.

Can you imagine what happened when Lenin finally came face to face with God?

He had one friend, his wife Krupskaya. That was all he needed, and more than he deserved. She stayed with him through all manner of humiliation, even through his open affair with Inessa Armand.

I was not that lucky.

I don't think I have ever had a friend, except as a very young child. I have known many people who have made me happy for periods of time. I have been married twice and have had children, but I have never had a friend. I searched for friendship.

Why? It is impossible for a professional politician to have friends. If you talk frankly to someone, it will come back to harm you, maybe tomorrow, maybe years in the future. A politician can trust no one.

No one should trust a politician.

Marx had it right when he said that politics is nothing more than the oppression of one class by another for some gain. The political world, like nature, may look peaceful, but there is constant turmoil. Political agreements are promises meant to be broken, like prophesies of treachery.

I have known many great men. I've watched energy and genius, sloth and fraud. I have killed great men with casual indifference. They are more easily replaced than one can imagine.

I kill the brave ones because they pose the threat of independent thought. I kill the intelligent ones because they might figure out what has happened and what should happen. I kill the creative ones because they are unpredictable when their plans are stopped by my restrictions. I kill the most faithful ones because once faith is lost, no matter the reason, men seek vengeance for their deception. I kill the philosophers because they know the truth. I kill the Party theoreticians because they see my heresy. I kill the most gentle because they might attract individual support by their meek trustworthiness. I kill the strong out of fear and envy.

What was I left with for the selection of friends: only weak cowards, from whom I had nothing to fear, but for whom I had only loathing and distrust.

Operating a large government is a difficult task requiring a lot of people to process and categorize ideas and activity. But running the government is a simple matter. I have done it alone, by unlimited force.

You don't have to be brilliant, vital, brave or honest. In fact, all those qualities hurt. You have to be sly, tactical, amoral, and ready to run away. You have to recognize your insatiable greed for material comfort and raw power, and your fear of being ousted.

You have to be a politician. If you are a professional politician, you can run the largest government by yourself by wiggling power, like bait, under the noses of the most incompetent, the most lustful of bureaucrats.

Professional bureaucrats are voracious consumers of society's worth. They leave nothing behind, except harm. They contribute nothing. They live for themselves all the while claiming to toil for the masses.

But they know their limits. They understand and respect the compulsion of their desires. They will do anything for you if you reward them. Never give them satisfaction, never give them "enough." As soon as a bureaucrat is content, he will build a cocoon to wall off the real world. He'll be of no service to you.

But tantalize him with delights - power - and his appetite may grow beyond any expectation, turning the humble bureaucrat into a voracious, unstoppable monster. Keep this man under your command. He is your attack dog, your vicious agent. He is your offensive weapon.

Groom him by making him more vicious.

When he is absolutely consumed with your patronage, kill him. He is now at the edge of control. As a politician, you must be in complete control. Once you elevate the most greedy and the most amoral to new levels of depravity, be aware they will look at you with tiger eyes, jumping through your hoops, but building enough familiarity to kill you with their contemptuous, unforeseen blow.

The only man in the Party whom I genuinely admired was Sergei Kirov.

In 1932, I wanted to give up the drudgery of the General Secretary's position and pass it on to someone I could handle. By then, I had amassed my core of loyal bureaucrats throughout the Party and government.

Kirov had worked for me throughout the Revolution. He was as brutal as me when the chips were down. I offered him the post.

He declined, saying he was more valuable in Leningrad where he could keep counterrevolutionaries at bay. I asked him several times. He gave me the same response. To be frank, after 1929, I didn't ask anyone for anything more than once.

I knew I couldn't trust him any longer because he was afraid of me for all the right reasons. I would have expected the Party and the organs to run perfectly. Any failure would have required his demise.

I wanted to do other, more personally interesting things with my time, such as hunting. When I realized Kirov was resisting my will, he had to die. Resistance, once declared, is intolerable. It must be contained and eliminated before it can spread.

I offered him the post. He refused. I offered him

power. He refused. I offered him material wealth beyond comprehension in the Soviet Union, hastening the arrival of personal Socialism for him. He refused. He was shot by an assassin on December 1, 1935. After I had him shot, I used the occasion of his murder to wipe out all his friends and a few of my enemies on the theory that there was a massive plot against me and the Party in Leningrad. I had the boys set up a few trials. The accused all gave correct testimony. They were mostly shot. If they hadn't cooperated in the trials, I would have shot their families, too.

I had the Chief of the NKVD, Henrik Yagoda, do a lot of the coordination and fabrication of evidence. He was very good at it. He was so good that I threw him into the third Kirov trial as an accused conspirator, and had him shot, replacing him with Lavrenti Beria. Yagoda surprised me with his intelligence and attention to detail. For that, he died. Beria, a scatterbrained rat, was a safe chief of the secret police. I had nothing to fear from him because he was incompetent.

But Kirov, poor Kirov, I liked him. He was handsome, energetic and so very Russian. All the boys liked him. I think he was being sincere when he said he wanted to work harder for me in Leningrad than he possibly could in Moscow as Party Secretary. It was only a matter of time until he realized he could work harder still for himself, for his own career, for his prominence over me. It was only a matter of time until he came for me! If I liked him so much, then I knew the rest of the boys must have admired him.

That alone was his downfall. If he were dumb, ugly and a thug, I could have trusted him.

I was looking at a picture the other day, from the

old days. A group of the boys and I were photograph-
ed in front of a bust of Lenin. Here is what happened
to that group.

Orjonikidze killed himself in 1937 because I had
the Cheka arrest and torture his brother, looking for
any confession they could come up with. I did the
same thing to various family members of my closest
associates to provoke unveiled revenge, rather than
wait for plots to hatch. Orjonikidze was weak. He felt
guilt. If he didn't kill himself, I would have had him
shot for lack of Revolutionary zeal. I let his brother
go: right to the gulag.

Kalinin was a repugnant, typically ignorant theore-
tician who reminded me of Lenin with hair. He constantly chain smoked rough cigarettes. Quite annoying.
I had to work very hard in 1936 to set up several
public trials. Kalinin tried to save a few of the defen-
dants from death, but without my approval. He
developed cancer in 1939. He was supposed to be
dying, so he retired from active politics. The little wind
bag hung on, so I had the Cheka shoot him in late
1941. We announced his death after the War.

Kirov, I have mentioned.

Kuibischev was killed by Yagoda in 1935 on my
orders. Kuibischev became a nuisance. Worse, he
harbored sympathy for internationalism. In the empire,
there was room for one "ism," Stalinism.

Voroshilov was one of the dumbest men I had
met, but he knew it and made no pretense to leadership. On the other hand, he was one of the most
vicious. Therefore, he fit my mold for the New Soviet
Man perfectly, and he remains alive today. The only
time I was tempted to shoot him was at the start of
the Great Patriotic War, when he almost lost it as our

brilliant general. He was an oaf. If I had him shot for
his mistakes, then people might ask where I was as the
national leader when the mistakes were made. I let
him live. I look at him sometimes and wonder what he
would be doing if not for my patronage. In the West,
he would be a machine politician, someone put forward with words placed in his mouth, engineered
political campaigns and promises to take care of campaign supporters. I guess, he's be in exactly the same
position, but not in military uniform. He'd be a civilian
defense minister. I don't think he could hold a real
job, not that he is nervous, like Lenin was, just that
poor Voroshilov doesn't have much on the ball. Maybe
he could write books.

Kagaonovich has a brain like a bug. If I call, he
jumps. I have had him watching that fat Ukrainian,
Khrushchev. Kagaonovich is harmless. Everyone thinks
he is quite dumb - they're wrong. He's worse. He's a
shrewd brute. I send him travelling to get reports of
how things are really shaping up around the empire.
He tells me it's great. The mere fact he makes it back
from these trips affirms my belief that I am in complete power. I don't care what he reports. His return
is the report. No matter where he goes, "it's great."

My present successor is Malenkov, not that it
means anything. I have another purge in the works
and this time, I intend to really clean house, more than
in 1938 and 1939. Malenkov will go. Bulganin will go.
Beria will go. They are getting too comfortable, and
they are getting together too much. They look hungry,
like fearful plotters.

The Politburo was created by Lenin as an elite
council of the men who controlled real power in the
Soviet Union. Lenin did not use it as a forum for

discussion, nor as an advisory body. He didn't like getting advice. He knew it all. He liked having powerful people where he could see them, but for the wrong reason.

Lenin liked to show off. He would gather the Politburo and then lecture for an hour about a meaningless point of Marxism. It was usually something he made up. He didn't ask for reports because he didn't want to be bogged down with detail.

I use the Politburo for a different purpose. It is still made up of the men who control some power, but only I control the real power. I get them together to listen to them. Once in a while, I have something to say, but I'd rather listen. I expect harmony - with me. I don't care what they say about each other, but when I get them together, I listen very closely.

Any deviation from doctrine results in a bullet. But I listen for more subtle things. I observe moods. I look to see who is friends with whom. I look for initiative, competence, assurance and creativity in thought - all of which are dangerous. If I find it - I remove it. Understanding this, modern Communists have a very professional face and a private face. At Politburo meetings, I see the professional face.

When I get them drunk at my dacha or when we stay over in the Kremlin offices through the night, I see their private faces.

In the seminary, I learned that, when drunk, men profess. Liquor loosens tongues. So I get the boys drunk and I listen. One of my standing rules is that all Politburo members have to be hard drinkers, like me.

It works.

Don't think that Communists are all dull. It's a public image. In private, they are like everyone else, which is part of the problem. They are just like everyone else who wants absolute power in government. To my eye, with the exception of a few mid east oil kingdoms, no one else has that kind of power! That's the real problem with Communists.

I am the only control in the whole system.

Georgians live for a long time. A very long time. I've looked into it. Some live for up to 130 years, far beyond the lifetimes of ordinary men. That makes me about middle aged. If I can keep myself in good shape, then I have to keep the dogs at bay, to stay alive. As soon as I relax, they'll kill me. So, I'll kill them first. Who'll be left? Me, which is all that counts.

It's time to gut the Politburo, the Red Army, the Party and the organs again.

That's why a politician cannot have a friend. If a friend sees weakness, he will render assistance. In politics, if a fellow politician sees weakness, he will circle for the kill, waiting, measuring, stalking - all the while with a smile and embrace for the common cause.

There are few rules in politics, because simplicity brings strength. But, I have a few:

1. Suppress courage and skill; promote cowardice and ignorance.

2. Promote enemies, then shoot them.

3. Keep shifting subordinates around, then shoot them.

4. Use as many foreigners as possible for your top subordinates, then shoot them.

5. Promote fear; encourage greed.

6. Steal as much as you can, while you can, before they shoot you.

Perhaps, if I do retire, I can become a professor. Of late, I have found myself thinking and acting more and more like a dogmatic iconoclast, hardened in irrational stubbornness. I could therefore teach economics, either in the West or within the empire. I prefer to remain in the empire, however, because there are too many Marxists in Western universities. In fact, the only Marxists left in years to come may exist in the reactionary towers of academia, long after the masses have thrown off the Party's yoke because they have experienced the bankrupt failure of real Socialism.

I've had enough of Lenin and Marx for this lifetime. And the next.

Koba
15 January 1953

CHAPTER SIXTEEN

WHAT MUST BE DONE

I plan on living a long time. A really long time.

But, God's plans count, not mine. I am not feeling especially well, and, judging from the way I look in mirrors versus the way I used to look in photos, I am not doing well. If I trust myself to my doctors, they'll probably kill me. If I trust my Lieutenants, they'll kill me. If I trust the Church, they might kill me. I'm not sure. I have given them a very hard time, and I'm not unjustly afraid of priests.

A priest can perform an act of violence and repent in confession, wiping the slate clean, perhaps of me! The modern Church is so modest. The ancient Church was led by warrior-clergy who could wield a sword from experience. I have to be careful.

Whenever I go, the empire will go. There is no one like me waiting to come forward. An empire cannot exist by voluntary participation. It works by force, constant deadly force applied from above on the subjects below. The minute the pressure stops, the empire crumbles.

I can be as violent as I want within segments of the empire, because the other segments have no sympathy for the present victim. It's true on a personal level. Divide and Conquer. If you are brutalizing one part of the organization, be generous with others. Their turn will come.

Always think out your plans and act with secrecy and surprise. This is not just military doctrine. It is true of any organizational oppression. Observe. Think out what must be done next, and do it. Don't forecast it unless you mean to extract opinions from possible objectors.

To find out who objects to your ideas, have someone else beside you make the announcement of a proposed action - preferably someone who is not individually powerful. Note the voiced opposition. Encourage it. Draw it all out from beneath every rock, within every shadow or from every tower. Now you know who your enemies are. They might not speak against you directly, in which case you might have to guess, but they may forget caution and speak against your stooge. Now you know. When you have the chance, take revenge.

I know how to work the system because it is my system. But, who will be able to work it after me? When I pass, it's over. In the ensuing turmoil, anything is possible, ranging from reformation (counterrevolution) to military extremism (expansion).

But, I won't be there to see it. I'll be dead.

I could take steps to so confuse the empire that it would shatter when I died, or I could just coast along and die, leaving the empire to flounder like a ship in a storm, heading for rocks in due time, manned by a crew of little courage and less wisdom.

To inherit my success, you have to be like me. I honestly think a man like me is unique. There has been no one like me since the great Kahn. Perhaps we occur every six hundred years to give birth to legend and warnings of what might transpire if absolute power is given, or stolen by any man.

My methods work to build an empire. They help to run it. We're broke, but I keep it going with the currency of human life, perhaps our greatest natural resource. I am willing to steal the product of workers, farmers and intellectuals, and use it for the benefit of the empire. But, that can only go on for so long, before the nation is completely bankrupt, even of people.

I have always made sure that there is bread in Moscow. Years ago, I starved the Ukraine to feed Moscow. When there is nothing left to steal from any part of the empire, then Moscow will starve. When that occurs, the people will take to the streets, with nothing to lose. The real question will be: will Russian troops fire on Russians for me or anyone else?

In 1917, the army turned on its Tsar. The Red Army remains the Russian Army, despite my efforts to make it loyal solely to me. I can't kill them all. So my successors have an impossible situation. They must either continue my example, which they can do for only a short time, or they must face the inevitable.

The empire must die. It must break up into pieces moving among and apart from each other. The West will have to rescue the empire from anarchy with money. Western wheat will fill their bellies, else they will go hungry. Western machines will renew the factories that are already crumbling.

Resistance? Of course. My Bolsheviks will resist to the last because they have enjoyed privilege beyond measure. My guess is that the empire will crumble when the last of the Old Bolsheviks goes.

But in death, I will still strike out. If my methods will expire in the empire's politics they will live on in Western business. Lies, extortion, fraud and theft are alive and well in the money centers in the West.

Who is going to pay for World War Two? No one. Who is going to pay for the war in Korea? No one.

The bills will never be paid. Debt is addictive. Once people get used to living with debt, once they can accept debt as a natural element of their national politics, they will never want to pay. Moral corruption accompanies debt. It is perfected when a nation refuses to repay its debt, choosing to burden its children with a present responsibility. Parents who deliberately harm their children are using my methods in personal application. Forcing children to pay the parents' political debt is one of my primary instruments of terror. Making children pay for economic excess is the Western equivalent.

That is national theft. The odd part is that it is theft from the nation itself. No one is paying debts. They just print money. Even though I have wished at times that the Rouble was worth something in international value, it has been just as well - we have commodities, not debts.

I have pressed the national insurgencies under my control to insist their local governments increase spending through the use of debt, arguing that present social emergencies require use of immediate debt.

There are always present emergencies. Something dire is always afoot. I can influence the budgets of nations by forcing them to become humanitarians. They will have to expand their budgets by taxing their economies for no productive purpose. The seduction for politicians is the lining of their own pockets and the perpetuation of their own careers. Lenin would never understand. He would want to bang heads and force-feed his ideas to people. I watch and observe. Then I use weakness for my advantage, without caring if people agree with me or not.

If I can get them to spend, they will continue to use debt, just as in the War. When they can't repay it, or when they repudiate their debt, their economies will crash. If I can get these fools to crash their mighty economic engines, there will be no bread in London or New York.

Then, they're mine.

The Red Army is a visible instrument of power, but it is not the most powerful. The mind is.

I'm currently funding 150 peace movements, all around the world. I attack Western governments every day through these movements. I've learned that Western governments kneel to constant, often subtle, political pressure, not to military challenge. If I keep repeating that I am a peaceful man, I will probably get a Nobel Peace Prize. Repetition, like chanting, soothes the mind. It persuades. It wins out where an army might fail. It supplies easy answers to difficult questions. Chanted propaganda.

The Berlin Airlift and the Marshall Plan were American programs that provided food for Europeans under my threat of invasion after the War. It was paid for with debt. Who will pay for it?

The time will come when the West will be drowned in debt, its own debt. Western nations and businesses will owe extraordinary amounts to each other in an interrelated web of debt. When they can't or won't pay, the web will unravel.

I'll be there.

When governments oppress their businesses and citizens with high taxes intended to pay for politically contrived, meaningless spending programs, economies will be crash. The politicians will scramble.

But, I'll be there.

When I was writing the Soviet Constitution in 1936, I read the original works of Thomas Jefferson and James Madison, Americans from Virginia. I studied in great detail, absorbing timeless ideas held by men of action. In the course of my reading, I also found the farewell address of George Washington. I'm relieved that no one reads their works any longer. Washington warned Americans to beware foreign entanglements and oppressive governments. Now they can't resist.

Washington was right. I quoted a part of Washington's speech to Roosevelt in a private discussion at Yalta. He recognized it after a few lines, and told me he wished Washington's advice could be employed in the twentieth century. Then he gave me Poland.

War is fought with subterfuge, by innuendo, through constant pressure. It need not be overtly violent to be completely effective.

Proponents of massive debt are my soldiers in a new form of economic war. If they slacken their binge, I'll force them to spend more by banging my military drum, setting the pace. Another forty years and they're mine. I'll only be 113 years old, which for a Georgian, is time for early retirement.

Then I can teach economics. The continuing question is, to whom?

Koba
1 March 1953

CHAPTER SEVENTEEN

IF...

Once, when I was in my twenties, I was in Siberia in the midst of another stretch of exile. I'd been picked up because the Okhrana in Petrograd knew me. My picture was in every police station.

Winter.

Siberia has two seasons - winter and a short, humid summer. The summer is unbearable because of the flies - not the heat. When the snow melts, water collects in puddles and ponds. The frozen ground becomes mud because the soil thaws less than a meter down. The deeper ground is permanently frozen. It's wet clay on ice.

The flies gather on your face. They form covers over your eyes, fill your nose and will clog your throat if you open your mouth to breathe. The mosquitoes are almost as bad, but the flies push them aside to get at you. We wore nets over our faces, even indoors, for sleeping.

Better the winter.

No insects.

Early winter, September, bears heavy snow, but without the overpowering wind that comes later, in November. If you have them, skis are quite useful in

September. The fir forests remain deep green from summer as the first snow comes down. The hunting is at its best because the animals, like the forest, are still lush from summer's bounty.

I used to travel on my skis, rifle over my shoulder, my greatcoat snugly closed with a triple rope coil around my waist. My legs were wrapped in layers of cloth. I had an old, American single-shot breech loader that fired a .58 caliber bullet. The rifle was heavy, long barrelled, and very accurate out to 500 meters. I was a pretty good shot.

I'd take bits of paper, bread and animal fat in a leather wrapping. Because the forest was not hard frozen in September, I could make a small fire for warmth, to melt ice for tea, and to keep wolves away if I passed a night in the snow. To make a fire, I'd gather wood, rub fat against the sticks, then ignite pieces of the paper with sparks from my flint. I had a few matches, but that was always a last resort. Matches were valuable - they were priceless at times because they represented the warm difference between life and death.

I carried a cast off bayonet which I had honed to a razor edge. I used it as a hunting knife and wore it at my right side. My food and gear were carried within two rolled blankets that I wore across my chest, over the shoulder, then tied together by my right hip.

My right arm powered my one ski-pole on the cross country trips; the left arm was only for balance. I wrapped my head in a large scarf, and sped across the flats or gingerly walked the forest tangles, skis over my right shoulder.

Eight bullets. Like matches, they were the difference. Life or death. The casings, which could be re-loaded, were precious in the wilderness.

A hundred kilometers. Sometimes I'd travel, guided by the early winter sun and the night stars, moving in an arc to return to my starting point. The world was made of open white fields, dangerous streams, great, majestic fir trees and stars that lit the snow with inspiration, even when the moon was absent.

There is a very fast deer, a cousin of the reindeer, only smaller, that I wanted to take. We called them "kidushkas." They're hard to track because they graze among trees. Their prints are soon covered by fresh snow and packed ice that drops from tall firs when the wind blows. Eventually, the deer form herds and migrate south, away from the severe cold. Large arctic wolves also hunt them.

I found very fresh kidushka droppings and stalked a small area of forest for two days, waiting, looking. They can stand still, almost next to you, but you won't see them unless you know what to look for. The snow lies on their golden backs, a natural camouflage. They blend into the forest's defensive embrace of color and shape. The hunter must be still and wait. Open your senses to the forest, and look for their sign.

You can see them breathe.

Their breath is made of warm mist, like yours. It carries on the cold air as though a small cloud, dissolving after travelling a few feet.

No, you can't hear them. The forest is filled with wind sound. You can't sneak up on them as they graze, because they'll smell you or hear your footfalls with their extremely sensitive ears.

As I stood still one late afternoon, the sun began to set in a purple sky, signalling time to depart my stand and build a shelter. I was cold, through and through. My muscles ached from holding the heavy rifle at the ready. My fingertips were covered in cloth, still, they felt the cold of the rifle barrel and trigger guard come through.

My shelter would be made of a snow wall built against the front of a fir covered lean-to. Once out of the wind, with a small fire, some hot tea, and maybe something to eat, it wouldn't be so bad. Later, when winter really arrived, it would be impossible. But now, it would be pleasurable.

The prospect of sleep was appealing. I had a bit of bread left. The night promised to be clear with those magnificent, limitless stars.

I saw his breath, a mist close to the ground, behind trees with low brush at the base, 75 meters away! The hunter waits; no movement, no sound, measured breathing. Bring the rifle around to aim slowly. The heavy bullet would shoot true, even through light brush. All I needed was a flash of target and I would take him down. It might be a darting face through the brush, a shoulder passing beyond cover, a tail - something to let me know the position of the animal's vitals.

As soon as I saw him, I'd take him. If I had to, I'd fire based on my guess of his position - if I saw his moving breath again! But I hated to waste a bullet. I hated to waste the shot and scare off all the game in the area.

The rifle hurt my back with its weight and froze my fingers as I gripped the trigger guard. I felt it, but the excitement of the moment took away the discomfort. My left arm served as a rest, because I couldn't use that hand to grip. My senses were out in front, probing, listening, touching that brush, almost tasting the prey. He would wait and hide. I had to take him from the protective shield of the forest.

No. I was wrong!

A reddish grey shape burst from the brush cover toward me, his long snout snarling, showing fanged teeth meant for one thing - killing. He came at speed, surprising me. As he galloped forward in powerful, lengthening strides, his breath burst out in clouds of steam, as though he was a hot engine bringing me death, charging through soft snow.

I gritted my teeth, cleared my aim and shot him as he was half way through his final jump at my throat. The heavy bullet caught him in his heaving breast, smashing him back in a screaming somersault.

Wolves, stalking me!

I turned fast, dropping my spent rifle, and grabbed my bayonet, knowing there would be at least one more. There was, coming in stride at me as had his brother. I ran at him. If you wait, you die. A wolf hits with 50 kilos of violence, sound and deadly purpose.

It doesn't matter how fast you are moving. Attack! Even bare handed, attack! When he jumps, lunge at him, hitting as hard as you can. I was lucky. I had run four or five steps and hit him with my head tucked down, my left shoulder, covered with my blanket roll as a shield, taking the blow.

My bayonet caught his gut and ripped him open as we fell. The struggle went on. I stabbed and struck, he bit and clawed my coat, tearing out the left shoulder padding after biting through the blankets.

Then he lay back, panting, wailing.

I killed him with my bayonet.

There were more. There are always more. They would be getting ready to move in, this time all together. I stumbled back to my rifle and loaded a bullet with my shaking hand which was slippery with the wolf's blood. I fired. The sound echoed, keeping the pack at bay. I had to move fast.

Immediately, I started a fire using matches and pieces of fir branches. It took, and soon I had quite a blaze going. I built a wall of fire behind and beside me with anything that would burn - branches, twigs, brush. As the fire grew, it consumed even wet wood. The fire's cracking was a welcome sound of protection. There was no further attack. They were still out there. They would wait all night if they had to. I loaded my rifle and extended the fire line.

I moved slowly, carefully, and dragged the wolf I had shot into my ring of fire. I dressed him down in the snow and roasted his hinds. I threw the rest into the blaze. The aroma would draw predators from all over the region, from bears down to foxes, bringing more prey to the wolves, tempting larger antagonists.

I ate the hinds fast, gathering strength. Two of my teeth were loosened by the struggle. I used snow to stop the bleeding where the second wolf had battered my left cheek through the protecting scarf. I noticed my right ring finger was broken, pushed away from the others at an odd angle. I didn't feel pain - there was no time.

As darkness was about to settle, I dropped a final load of brush onto the fire and dumped the other, gutted wolf into the flames. I gathered my gear and moved away from the fire, risking further attack in pursuit of a safe height. Leaving my rifle at the base of a large fir, I climbed - I dragged myself up into the swaying, snowy branches and tied myself to the trunk with the rope that had held my coat closed. My energy was spent. I was empty.

After a short while, I saw stalking wolves, shadow monsters against the red fire glow that swept the snow with harsh, flickering light. They came closer and closer to the flames, sniffing the ground, then the tips of the carcasses that stuck out of the burning branches. Frantic wolves circled, tasting the air with their hunting instinct, but the aroma of burning flesh dominated their tracking sense, as I had hoped. They couldn't concentrate. I fell asleep as they raced in the confused fury of frustrated revenge and growing, insatiable hunger for my flesh.

I awoke. It was the next day, about mid-afternoon according to the sun's position. I had slept for a very long time. My bones and joints were stuck, frozen from the cold and the intense combat with the charging wolf. Movement was painful, unsure. The blaze was only smoldering. No animals were in sight. Wolves could not get up into the trees, but if they had stayed they would be right below, confident in their numbers, reckless in their group strength. I was alone.

There was a blood taste in my mouth. I was covered in soft snow.

I had to leave or die in that tree. The descent was long, excruciating. Once down, I grasped my rifle like a crutch and staggered forward, stretching my cramped, locked legs, moving to the hot ashes. The carcasses were gone, eaten somewhere in the brush. Bears? Cannibal wolves?

I stood still, staring, the circulation returning to my toes and fingertips. Gentle snow fell, covering the night's violence, removing its fierce desperation. From the corner of my eye, I caught movement. Far off, 80 meters to my left, a beautiful, snow-flecked deer walked across a small clearing. I watched him sniff the air then tilt his head, puzzling over the fire smell. He caught my scent and bounded to cover. I didn't bring the rifle up. Didn't want to. Probably couldn't, anyway.

I skied home, slowly, gratefully. No matter how painfully each movement resisted, I was alive! The scratch marks near my neck, the broken finger, the deep bruises and frostbite eventually healed, leaving only a few scars. I continued to stalk forests while my body regained its strength. The deer were safe.

Thereafter, I hunted wolves.

When I gather the Politburo these days, I listen. I watch. Power is a forest.

I remain the hunter.

If that wolf had not taken a last, full breath before charging...

Koba
2 March 1953

EPILOGUE

PRESSING BUSINESS

(by the author)

I'm in a rush to catch a plane and head south on an unexpected trip. Events have taken on lightening speed and good fortune. Resolution, often elusive, is at hand, perhaps giving rest to the pain of many crimes. Let me explain.

This book has explored the past tumult of ideological and violent history during a period the world might want to forget, but never will.

In the meanwhile, Mikhail Gorbachev, President of the Soviet Union and, hopefully, the final General Secretary of the Communist Party of the Soviet Union, Bolsheviks, has received the Nobel Peace Prize for 1990. The last Communist leader to be so honored was Le Doc Tho, one of the wartime leaders of North Vietnam who made a fool out of Henry Kissinger during the useless Paris negotiations to end that tragic war.

Mikhail is called "the Boss," in the intelligence business. It's not an honor. If he was fat, they would call him, "slim." If he were stupid, he's be known as "Einstein." The boys deal in private humor. Nicknames are not used in reports, but they are heard in the highest level discussions. Official code names are used in all written reports, where very little humor resides.

The Boss has a lot of problems.

There have been bread shortages in Moscow, along with increasing shortages of everything else. If there is not enough fuel to heat Moscow's vast tenements in the cold of winter, perhaps the population will take to the streets with the politician's worst nightmare - the rope.

Worst enemy? There is no double talk, no pay off that corrupts the rope. It means summary justice. It means the final defeat of personal power - until the new class of power emerges.

In the back of every politician's mind there is a dread that he will be discovered for the hollow shell he is, and then - the rope.

When the population has nothing to lose, when things get so bad that death might be preferable to life, the Bolsheviks will have to face the old question: will the Red Army fire on civilians? Russian civilians. Is there a Father Gapon, ready to march tomorrow across Red Square? Is there a Trotsky ready to grab power if Mikhail fires on the crowds?

Is there a rope for the Boss and the rest of the scum. Or will they be shot like the Romanovs, their bodies dumped into a well in some remote region?

There is certainly no Trotsky in the Politburo today. There is no Stalin to make the decision and start the killing.

Today's Red Army will not fire on Russians. It's a topic of discussion in every military post. Duty - yes, without question. Murder - no. No way. They mean it.

If the Party tried to bring in Asian troops who

might not care about killing ethnic Russians, the traditional Red Army Command Staff, which is, for all purposes, the Mother Russian Army, wouldn't sit still.

That means civil war. It's coming fast.

Who would feed the population? What would happen to the rest of the world?

During the first Revolution, that "rest of the world" ignored Russia until it was too late. Then, after the First World War, the West first acted to punish the Reds. Later, politically, the West acted as if the Reds didn't exist, denying diplomatic recognition and trade.

Things have changed.

The Russians control the largest stockpile of nuclear weapons on the planet. They have delivery systems that can hit the US and the rest of the industrialized world, including China, Japan and India, with ease. Lately, they have pulled a lot of the nuclear munitions home, back from Eastern Europe and even from republics within the Soviet Union that are getting edgy.

The Soviets are worried.

Exactly who controls Soviet nuclear forces? The Communist Party? For how long? They can't get rid of their nukes. We, in the West, cannot grab them and destroy the arsenal.

In 1921, Trotsky could not reach out with the Red Army and strike the shores of the United States. Today, as I write this, a Soviet nuclear-powered submarine armed with nuclear weapons cruises the Atlantic within 400 miles of my home in Virginia. There is usually one up by New York City, too. The warning time from launch to surface impact is under 2 minutes.

The missile launching subs used to go on station

closer in, but the key is not miles: the key is time. Weapons systems have improved that much. There is no escape from a low flying, submarine launched cruise missile armed with a nuclear warhead.

We are living in a kind of Germany, you see. Go back in time to 1935. The power map of Europe, and even the world, showed England and France on the western edge. Germany was in the middle. Russia was on the eastern edge. Those were the Great Powers.

Today, China is the western edge, the United States is in the middle, and the Russians are on the eastern edge. In between are various trouble makers, whether it be Iraq or the Punjab.

We, in the United States, should be very concerned about the Russians, because the Revolution is not over; it is changing. There are pockets of resistance, and, as I found out, little bureaucratic fortresses of traditional power, surviving like dinosaurs until today. The question of succession is open; the fact of nuclear power is reality.

I met a friend the other night for drinks in the Artillery Bar, near 20th and K Street in the District. Open all night. It's in the basement of an office building. The Artillery has a deserved reputation for hospitality to the people who loyally serve through the nights when rugged professionals run the Federal Government.

The clam chowder is excellent. I appreciate the subtle spice and the smooth warmth of Chef Tito's old reliable. To order the house specialty, you ask for a cup or bowl of "smash." Tito then dumps in a few shots of very strong brown rum, a tablespoon of sugar, and serves the potent chowder up with a freshly cut onion on the side. It goes well with hot sake. It is the best chowder in the world, east or west.

My friend was Air Force alumni. He called me at the office and invited me for a liquid dinner.

He works these days on the US Customs Service payroll, active in the useless interdiction war against drugs. But his brother, who appears on no one's payroll, is a hard core spook who works with satellite photographic intelligence in the big boiler room in Maryland.

Supposedly, the spook brother heard a story from one of his colleagues who works on electronic communication interceptions. The spook brother passed it to his drug enforcement brother who was about to pass it on to me.

It was no secret: when FX died, I made inquiries for information about who had done it. I knew it was the Russians, and I knew why, but I literally wanted to know who. A name. The inquiry was a little unusual because it was blunt. As a civilian, I could do that. Governments speak more softly, always leaving room for the responding party to somehow negotiate. No me. Not this time.

If I didn't get names, I'd start taking them out, wherever I might find them. So, they'd have to come back and finish up. It gets messy. No mater what, they would have to deal with me.

The Artillery was one-third full. All men. It was 2:30 AM. We sat, tenderly spooning our smash over and over to keep the mixture of alcohol and soup consistent. The hot rum aroma was delicious by itself. We talked for a little while about life, places we had both toured.

"Your name came up in the mail yesterday," he said, matter of factly, followed by a small sip of soup.

"My brother tells me it was just an in-house blip, routine, limo to limo hot telephone." He looked at me with a little smile. "And I thought you were back in the law business," he mocked me.

"Where," I asked.

He resumed spooning the soup. "Zilville." The Politburo members still use big Zil Limousines for transport around Moscow. Like hotshots around the world, they love to show off their power by talking to each other over car telephones. The transmissions are officially supposed to be secure, scrambled. They're not. It's difficult to scramble a transmission against a dedicated intercept run by computers.

Scramblers are not static.

Sophisticated scramblers randomly mix signals with no predictable order by using a computer chip. The chip performs virtually infinite choices for frequency changes and transmission interrupts. All the chips in Zilville can be changed at almost the same time by technicians, thus making their car telephones a very private network. To dial in, one needs a compatible chip.

To intercept, a fast computer reviews the live or taped signal and, in micro seconds, tries various probabilities against each bit of scrambled information. If the scrambler works at high speed, the grabber must work at ultra high speed. The present technology difference between Russian scramblers and US grabbers is exponential. Their equipment is good - against the third world. Ours is so far advanced, there is no comparison.

Our people have to slow down their machines to wait for the lagging output of the Russian gadgets. The Russians know this and they don't talk about anything of real importance on their car telephones. Because they know they are bugged long distance, a lot of what they say is disinformation.

They may discuss something, but it might not be true. It may be a careful attempt to plant a false idea in Western intelligence circles. We spend billions of dollars to gather dubious intelligence that we feel is probably disinformation and, therefore, worse than useless.

It sounds insane. But there is another use.

The Boss has problems with his people, many of whom hate him and look for opportunities to embarrass him at every turn. In order for the Boss to talk to the US or any other Western government, he has to go through his foreign ministry to arrange contact, even very secret contact. If he is working on a matter of the utmost confidentiality, he might go through the KGB. No matter what department he chooses, the Boss can't get through to the West without a lot of his uncontrollable people knowing.

Sometimes he wants privacy.

He gets it on the car telephone.

When he calls one of the Politburo, the Boss knows he is being picked up. By us. He uses it a lot.

The US State Department, many of whom are still in love with the romance of Communism, don't get their soft hands on the material until after it has run useful channels on the intelligence side of the executive branch of government. Within hours after the top secret intercepts are handed over to State, they reliably pop up at the KGB Headquarters outside Moscow. Funny how that happens. Then it gets around the Soviet Union's foreign and security ministries, where it bounces back again to the CIA within a few hours. Just so you know, if it gets to the British, it ends up for a second time back in Moscow within 1 day. It then bounces back to the CIA for a third time. There are leaks, spies, sympathizers and idiots everywhere in the bureaucracies.

When the Boss calls, he has a chance to talk with the US.

Direct. No interpreters, no staff, no composed papers.

I wasn't surprised that my name had come up, only that it had come up in a Zil.

My friend continued, "You asked about a friend of yours. Three fellows came over for the embassy tour two days before your friend died. One was a general, not just a mere colonel. They left the morning after the job, taking the Concorde out, yes, the very expensive Concorde, to Paris. Very unlike the boys to pay extra. Then they went right home. No R&R."

I was finishing my soup. I caught Tito's eye as he was strolling by in his kitchen whites, and waved for another two bowls with more onion. He waved back, with a fast thumbs-up, a wink, and a smile. He wore two hearing-aids that didn't do much for his almost total hearing loss. Hind Helicopter Gunships on a search-and-destroy mission had blown his hearing away, forever, several years ago in Afghanistan. He was teaching Afghan rebels how to use Stinger missiles against the fat choppers when his group was caught by a low flying squadron. He killed one Hind, damaged another, and ran like hell along the ridges and gullies of the notorious Koppur Pass for a full day to avoid the Spetsnaz troops that always mopped up for the Hinds.

I sat, listening as my friend continued.

"A lot of the Soviet big shots are getting ready to go. They have packed up, pushed money from all kinds of in-country sources into Swiss Accounts, and are shopping for real estate. You'll find this interesting - since the Generals have been tossed in Argentina, it's become a popular place for the Soviets. I would have thought Cuba, but they don't like Castro, and I think they have all had it with Marxism. At first, there was a little vacation traffic, then more. Now, they are buying the place up. I see some of the staff getting mixed up in the drug business. Never would have happened before."

Tito brought the smash, laid it out neatly before us, and took off the empties.

"So the news in Zilville is that the Boss was very mad at KGB General Idiot, and wanted him out of town fast before he had time to dump anyone else on the street in the District. Seems the boss had just found out."

I looked up from my soup into my friend's eyes and shrugged.

"Uh-huh. The Boss had just heard that someone was looking for information about General Idiot, and who the hell was this guy, this general to cause any trouble at a delicate time like this. The Boss wanted him fired, kicked out, chased out of town."

"That's all?" I asked.

"Not quite. They don't zap people as easily anymore -oh, did you hear? They did zap about twenty or thirty guys last week after something went wrong in a Rocket Forces exercise. No trial, no comment. Bang! The exercise wasn't scheduled. Something happened. Somebody switched on; no question. Took everyone by surprise and they're mad as hell. Losing

control. All that stuff. Anyway, this general gets fired,
and guess where he's going for retirement? Argentina."

"Where?" I interrupted.

He smiled. "Y'know, this message stuff is funny.
The Boss laid the whole thing out, as though saying if
you want him, you can have him. Yeah. They had a
series of houses in a mountain town outside Buenos
Aires called La Palazita. In the last two years, they've
bought big acreage nearby, probably for the main men
if it gets really tough at home. They bought it from
Germans who are dying off and need cash for old age
medical care as well as the increasing cost of
protection from the Israelis. So, after a glorious career
carrying the sword and shield for the Party, General
Idiot becomes their latin camp director. 'Fact, he's
probably there now. Well, tomorrow. They gave him a
day off en route."

"Who is this guy?" I asked.

"The Boss was upset, and, as you know, he tends
to blurt things out sometimes, spur of the moment.
The Boss said he was sick and tired of that rat
bastard's bastard son, the general. The guy's name is
interesting. Joseph Virlova. Well according to the Boss,
he's had it with the bastard son and doesn't care if his
mother, Magda Virlova, was the beautiful physicist
who assisted Sakharov in developing their H-Bomb.
She got a very quiet Hero of the Soviet Union for that.
But the Boss said something else that has the intercept
crowd chucking: how could she have that animal's
child? If he'd had his way, no child of Stalin's would
have been let live!"

I was stunned. I didn't need it repeated.

My friend had a little more to say. "So, the real
reason I am paying for your dinner is to tell you that

our friends think something is going on here and they'd like to talk to you about it. Virlova is young for a general. No one is quite sure how he came to his exalted position that fast without clear connections with a power faction. OK?"

Something was going on. Stalin had a bastard son! And all this time he'd been protected in the organs, right in the cowboy Fourth Directorate. No wonder things were breaking down. The Boss was in shaky control now - what about tomorrow? My mind was alive with the possibilities. Then the dangers. He was going to Argentina, but stopping somewhere first. A message? A warning!

"Hey, wyo," my friend said, using the familiar Sicilian for "kid." "I'm still here. Can you meet with the boys in a day for a full discussion?"

I snapped back into the conversation, but not to answer his question. "Did the Boss say where Virlova was going?"

"No. Just right out, don't wait for Aeroflot, which flies direct to New York every other day. Get him the hell out of the country, now. A short stopover - OK. Probably a girlfriend. Who knows. They just want him out, now."

I quickly thought of carriers who fly direct out of Moscow to the West. Only Aeroflot right now. Then there are one-stops on Air France, Pan AM, and Finnair! Forget Washington.

He wasn't interested in me, yet. If he showed up here, his embassy would call the Boss and then they would shoot him. No, it wasn't Washington.

One was Finnair!

He was still on business, out of control, even the Boss's control! That's why the Boss had called!

I told my old friend that I couldn't make the meeting, but that I would call him shortly. I bolted from the Artillery.

I got a cab and raced the few blocks to my office. I threw the driver a $20 bill and ran into the building, not waiting for the change. It was almost 4 AM, which made it late morning in Helsinki. I called Kerbusson.

Helsinki is on the direct dial networks.

I called his office and got his machine, time after time. I called his regular girlfriend and got her answering machine. I called his occasional girlfriend and got no answer.

It was Helsinki. "Jesus," I thought,"I got him into this." I called Malk, his home, his office all over again. Nothing. Where the hell was Mickie, his male secretary who came in for a few hours every day? If I flew over it would take 24 hours. If I asked my friends for cover, his part in the process would be disclosed and his life endangered all over again, maybe from my own crowd.

My stomach felt powerful tension, as though I would implode. I calmed myself and kept calling and waiting. Nothing.

Hours passed. At about 9 AM, after I had called, literally, a hundred times, I called his office and got a human answer.

It was Mickie.

All he said was a mumbled greeting. Instantly, I knew. I knew, I knew, I knew.

Mickie, a young college student with an outgoing sense of humor answered in a hushed tone.

We spoke in Finnish in quiet phrases.

"Kerbusson? He was on the way out to meet you about the new papers."

"Gone. Auto accident on the road to Malk. Hit and

run, knocked off the road. Burned..."

"Where was I? In Washington, of course. Supposed to meet him? In Malk?"

I didn't say no, just that I was held up and I was trying to contact Rik. I begged off and said I would call later.

He was gone.

Drawn to Malk by someone using my name.

****

I'm sitting at my desk, looking around the room, through eyes scratchy from lack of sleep. It's an odd sensation. I'd first heard from FX as I sat here one rainy night, not long ago.

Today, the sun promises to bathe Washington in delightful color. A pleasant breeze has come up. It pushes through my open window, making the venetian blinds shake occasionally.

I've made calls to reserve a Lufthansa flight out, tonight, and to round up travel papers. Oh, and some fishing gear.

It's fishing season in Argentina where their weather is the reverse of ours. Serious anglers, stalking mythical, gigantic rainbow and brown trout, come from all over the world to the mountains outside Buenos Aires. When fishermen travel, they caravan bags full of gear: nets, poles, rods, secret lures and attitudes of certain success. Unlike Iceland, Argentina doesn't require the sport fisherman to sterilize gear before entering the country.

Argentina says,"Welcome, bring whatever you want and spend a lot of money - please. Credit cards are fine. Just spend money!"

Fishermen are used to travelling alone, obsessed by the pursuit of trophies they can't see until the fish strikes the surface. It's not like hunting, where you stalk. With fishing, you know the prey is in the water, but you wait for him to come to you.

Virlova. La Palazita. It should be interesting. I plan to be back in 72 hours.

There is more material from Stalin's notes that will be published in the future as I have time to finish successive translations. I've decided to leave the Kerbüssøn chapter in the book, now that he is gone and cannot be hurt. I had written it, but was undecided about exposing his name - afraid of revenge against him.

A true heart commands. I must go.

I'm not going to make this trip entirely on my own. As this manuscript hits my editor's desk in a few hours and begins the long path to publication, I'll be heading south with a few old friends, some pretty rough company.

If I catch my prey, and I intend to, there won't be enough left to stuff.

Bank on it.

Adios!

EDITOR'S NOTE:
(by S. Kopf, A.F.S., Editor)

NEWS FROM ROME

It has been two months since Finegan left for Argentina. According to confidential sources, a Soviet citizen was found outside Buenos Aires, in La Palazita, shot so many times that physical recognition was not immediately possible. Based on wallet contents, his body was returned to the Soviet Embassy in Buenos Aires, examined, identified, and then transported back to Moscow by military aircraft with a special honor guard reserved for general officers. The Argentines termed it a robbery attempt and apologized for the unfortunate incident. General Virlova's family received the apology gracefully.

Under a postmark from Rome, Finegan sent a cryptic note in latin to the effect that, after a persuasive discussion with his newly found friend, he had learned of two promising opportunities that required immediate attention. I've no idea what he's doing.

He assured me he would return after that, apologized for the digression, and told me to go forward and print. So be it. I'm but a humble editor. Writers are such an aggravation!

A short quote from his letter follows, with the accompanying translation. He asked me to tell readers to mark the page, to return to it often.

The Latin:

"Illa praeclara, in quibus publicae utilitatis species prae honestate contemnitur.plena exemplorum est nostra res publica cum saepe, tum maxime bello Punico secundo; quae Cannensi calamitate accepta maiores animos habuit quam umquam rebus secundis; nulla timoris significatio, nulla mentio pacis. Tanta vis honesti, ut speciem utilitatis obscuret."

English Translation:

There are noble times in history where the apparent expediency of the state has been overruled out of regard for honor. Our country has many demonstrations to offer from her history, especially in the Second Punic War when the news broke about the disaster at Cannae. Rome displayed a greater courage than she ever did during victory. There was no trace of fear. There was never talk of a surrender. Honor is so powerful it subdues the specious appearance of expediency.

- Cicero, de Officiis.
His masterpiece.

ACKNOWLEDGEMENTS

I'm grateful for the inspiration of those who pulled me through the expedition described herein.

Many of those I would salute cannot be named because they work in the shadows or violated various bureaucratic prohibitions to pass sensitive information.

I can use trench names, but such "handles" can be deciphered. No vengeance is as salted as that of the bureaucrat scorned. No bureaucrats had a hand in this work.

I extend my hand to friends in Finland. I shall wait until forever to repay unknown mechanics who maintain the Zilville scramblers.

Can I applaud the inspiration of a man who has passed with sufficient vigor that it would add anything to the resonance of a life well lived? Old, friend, we shall meet again, perhaps to fish and hunt elsewhere.

I acknowledge my debt to soldiers who bear arms in defense of our Republic.

And for the Compania - you are in my daily prayers.

My friends, accept my gratitude. It runs without reservation. If I cannot use your names, I still owe you a big one.

Adios!

- PGF, Jr.

PATRICK G. FINEGAN, JR.

Critically acclaimed author of <u>MASTER YOUR STOCKBROKER</u> (WALL STREET SECRETS) and <u>MASTER FINANCIAL STATEMENTS</u> (WHO MURDERED SAVINGS AND LOANS?), Patrick G. Finegan, Jr. tackles formidable, controversial subjects head on, in the torrid arena of single intellectual combat.

He grew up in New York City, where he attended Jesuit schools. Finegan claims Latin classics changed his life, dissolving barriers between our circumstances and those of the past. He travelled widely in the US Air Force, then as a lawyer in the securities business. His books have received praise from major financial broadcasters for straightforward discussions of complex issues. Professional journals have reviewed his work in depth.

He lives in Virginia with his wife and children in the region trod by some of his personal heros: Washington, Jefferson, Madison, Monroe, and US Grant. He enjoys slamming a weight bag, Rickenbacker 12's, lawyering and writing. Additional books are "in the works," revisiting finance, and another historical novel.

In an epilogue to one of his financial books he said, "I am inspired by those who, facing challenge, act. Thoughts, without men who will stand for them, are meaningless." He means it.

He practices law in Washington, DC.

The Critics Choice:

MASTER YOUR STOCKBROKER

" I RECOMMEND THIS BOOK..." Bernard Meltzer, WOR Radio, New York City.

" A WONDERFUL BOOK..." Dick Sinclair, KIEV Radio, Los Angeles

" GET THIS BOOK..." Steven Conway, WINZ Radio, Miami.

" HIGHLY RECOMMENDED... " Bill Bresnan, WABC Radio New York City

" CLIENTS READING HIS BOOK ARE GOING TO BE ASKING THEIR BROKERS SOME UNCOMFORTABLE QUESTIONS (HE EVEN PROVIDES THEM WITH A LIST)." Registered Representative, the professional journal of the Securities Brokerage Industry. Five column review!

MASTER FINANCIAL STATEMENTS
Who Murdered Savings and Loans?

" WRITTEN IN A BREATHLESS POLEMICAL STYLE...SURE TO INFURIATE CONSERVATIVE ELEMENTS OF THE PROFESSION, BUT WILL STRIKE A SYMPATHETIC CORD WITH ANY NON-EXPERT..." Accounting Today, the news magazine of the Accounting Profession. FULL PAGE HEADLINE!

" PRAISEWORTHY!" Bernard Meltzer, WOR Radio, New York City.

" SEND FOR IT!" Bill Bresnan, WABC Radio New York City.